T0024531

The
Eye
Opener

The
Eye
Opener

Hazelden
Publishing

ISBN: 978-0-89486-023-2

Printed in the United States of America

PREFACE

(From the Second Edition of THE EYE OPENER)

"This little book is dedicated to the God of my understanding.

"Its purpose is to bring various phases of AA philosophy to the arrested alcoholic as interpreted and understood by the author. It is not in any sense official, for AA has no official opinion and each member speaks only for himself.

"The author of this poor work is neither a writer nor a scholar. His philosophy is not original and was gleaned from many sources.

"If some heart is made lighter, some home happier, or some soul strengthened, we will feel bountifully repaid for our efforts."

The publishers gratefully acknowledge the generosity of T. W. R.

THE TWELVE STEPS OF A.A.*

1. We admitted we were powerless over alcohol—
   that our lives had become unmanageable.

2. Came to believe that a Power greater than our
   selves could restore us to sanity.

3. Made a decision to turn our will and our lives ove
   to the care of God *as we understood Him.*

4. Made a searching and fearless moral inventory o
   ourselves.

5. Admitted to God, to ourselves, and to anothe
   human being, the exact nature of our wrongs.

6. Were entirely ready to have God remove all thes
   defects of character.

7. Humbly asked Him to remove our shortcomings

8. Made a list of all persons we had harmed, and be
   came willing to make amends to them all.

9. Made direct amends to such people wherever pos
   sible, except when to do so would injure them o
   others.

10. Continued to take personal inventory and whe
    we were wrong promptly admitted it.

11. Sought through prayer and meditation to improv
    our conscious contact with God *as we understoo
    Him,* praying only for knowledge of His will for u
    and the power to carry that out.

12. Having had a spiritual awakening as the result o
    these steps, we tried to carry this message t
    alcoholics, and to practice these principles in al
    our affairs.

The Twelve Traditions of A.A.*

1. Our common welfare should come first; personal recovery depends upon A.A. unity.
2. For our group purpose there is but one ultimate authority—a loving God as He may express Himself in our group conscience. Our leaders are but trusted servants—they do not govern.
3. The only requirement for A.A. membership is a desire to stop drinking.
4. Each group should be autonomous, except in matters affecting other groups or A.A. as a whole.
5. Each group has but one primary purpose—to carry its message to the alcoholic who still suffers.
6. An A.A. group ought never endorse, finance, or lend the A.A. name to any related facility or outside enterprise lest problems of money, property and prestige divert us from our primary purpose.
7. Every A.A. group ought to be fully self-supporting, declining outside contributions.
8. Alcoholics Anonymous should remain forever non-professional, but our service centers may employ special workers.
9. A.A., as such, ought never to be organized, but we may create service boards or committees directly responsible to those they serve.
10. Alcoholics Anonymous has no opinion on outside issues, hence the A.A. name ought never be drawn into public controversy.
11. Our public relations policy is based on attraction rather than promotion; we need always maintain personal anonymity at the level of press, radio, and films.
12. Anonymity is the spiritual foundation of all our traditions, ever reminding us to place principles before personalities.

* The Twelve Steps and Twelve Traditions reprinted with permission of A.A. World Services, Inc. Copyright © 1939.

Without the introduction of a purpose into our lives we would be but dried-up drunks, wallowing in self-pity for the loss of that which we were forced to deny ourselves in order to bring about some semblance of order in our lives. We would be "off the bottle" but not for a moment happy about it — never with any sense of security.

We who have found AA have introduced that something into our lives that enabled us, with the Grace of God, to "fix" ourselves.

We have not given up anything — we have acquired something; we are no longer frustrated people, because we have introduced into our lives a reliance in a Power greater than ourselves, that we did not have before. That Power has opened up a new way of life, free of worry, fear and frustration.

Probably in the history of the world no tyrant can be found who welded chains so strong upon his victims as did that "Ol' Debil Rum."

Even our most secret desires were controlled by his influence, and our families, our health and our very lives themselves were disregarded when opposed to the demands for a drink.

Fortunately for us in AA we still had a freedom of choice of master and when we decided to "turn our will and our lives over to the care of God", we accepted a new Master, one even more demanding than the first, but with this one vast difference — our chains were now bonds of love.

You can't tell a drunk anything, but you can show him. All too frequently, we cry out on Monday, attend our first meeting on Tuesday and try our hand at Twelve Stepping on Wednesday.

With a sketchy conception of what it is all about, with little or no knowledge of the Program, sometimes with the smell of paraldehyde still on our breath, we venture forth to dry up the world and when we fail we wonder why.

Remember the 12th step says, ''Having had a spiritual awakening as the result of these steps, we tried to carry this message to alcoholics.'' You can't carry the message before you receive it nor can you give it if you don't possess it.

Pride in ancestry has kept many alcoholics from the humbleness that is a prime requisite of success in our program. The deeper one is in his cups, the greater is his remorse for his condition — not because of his descent to the level of the animal, but because of his betrayal of his noble family traditions.

Ancestry is good only when it inspires living up to its traditions. When it becomes a throne built on other men's accomplishments it is nothing.

We alcoholics should be reminded of Voltaire's words when he said: "He who serves well has no need of ancestors."

Let us think less of our ancestors and more about what kind of ancestors we will make.

Living all the days of our lives, living them to their utmost; putting all our life into them; getting all the life that each day has to offer; this truly is living at its best, at its fullest.

Every day, then, will be fully lived — a grand succession of experiences both pleasant and unpleasant (for life is made up of both), and without the one the other would not be recognized or appreciated.

Live each day as though it were your last day on earth.

Let us stop and think about our room here on earth. We have occupied it all our lives; we have free heat and light. From the windows of this room we can look upon the grandest of nature's landscapes if we so desire but it also looks upon poverty, slums and filth, if that is what we have eyes for.

How can we pay for our Room on Earth? Only by serving our fellow men, the children of the Landlord, "and inasmuch as ye did it unto these, ye did it unto Me."

If you do less you are not worthy of your Room on Earth.

One day you were a weak, hopeless sot; then came a day when you were clear eyed and sober. You are certainly aware that you could not, of yourself, accomplish this miracle — for it was truly a miracle.

This did not happen because you were selected by wild chance. You were chosen because you possessed the qualities that made you suitable for the work the Higher Power needed done. To say that you lack the ability to "carry the message" is to question the wisdom of God.

There is work here that you were born to do.

God does not willingly inflict punishment on men. Our pain and our suffering are the direct results of a violation of the Moral, Natural or Civil Law.

We who were guilty of overindulgence must pay the price, not FOR our indulgence, but BECAUSE of our indulgence. The consequences must follow as the night follows the day. It is the LAW.

We have violated this LAW and we have paid dearly for it, but we do not have to persist in our violations. The body will heal, sins will be forgiven, things will right themselves if, and when, we put our thoughts and actions in tune with the immutable laws of God, of Nature and of man.

As sins bring punishment as a natural consequence, so right living brings its own compensations, not as a reward for good deeds done but as a CONSEQUENCE.

It would be most difficult to contradict the statement that you cannot get sobriety unless you honestly want it. You cannot find a God of your understanding unless you honestly seek Him. It is likewise true that you cannot reap full measure from our Program unless you honestly live it.

Self-deception is very hard to recognize for if we recognized it, it would no longer be deceptive. Honesty with ourselves can only be acquired by diligent study of ourselves, our ideals, our ambitions and our motives.

Alcoholism, or compulsive drinking, is incurable. We have seen too much evidence of the fact to believe differently — yet, occasionally, some of us get the idea that we are exceptions to the rule. Then the Rat Race begins all over again.

We are alcoholics. We must admit it and accept it as one of those things we cannot change.

If you have the brains of a bedbug you will admit that you were powerless over your drinking. You will recognize the fact that one day you were a drunk and then on the next day you were an ex-drunk.

Was it because one day you were weak and the next day you had become suddenly strong? You know better.

On that great day of reformation you sought refuge in a Power greater than yourself, which was even beyond your ability to visualize. That Power has been an ever-present source of help ever since.

If you are successfully practicing the Program, you have established a spiritual contact whether you are aware of it or not.

We brought nothing into this world and shall take nothing out. We are in the process of living a lifetime, one day at a time. It is therefore reasonable that we should gather as much of the richness of living from each day as we possibly can.

Does it make you feel good all over when you spend a buck or two on some poor devil? Then don't deny yourself this dividend of living.

In Matthew's account of the Sermon on the Mount he quotes Christ as saying "BE YE THEREFORE PERFECT, EVEN AS YOUR FATHER WHICH IS IN HEAVEN IS PERFECT."

Our first reaction is that that is impossible. Christ either did not say this or else He did not mean it.

If He didn't say it then the Bible is inaccurate. If He did and did not mean it, then Christ drops below Divine stature. No, He said and meant it. For man to aspire to less is a direct rejection of His order.

To cry that we are circumscribed by human limitations is to deny the God in us which makes all things possible.

We probably will never arrive at that state of perfection but we can, one day at a time, strive to attain that goal.

Within our ranks we have many faiths and creeds. All of us seek and find our Power greater than ourselves in our own way and give Him a personality according to our own understanding. Yet withal, we abide in peaceful toleration and respect the faiths that we each have found.

Even those of us who are still groping in uncertainty and doubt are gradually acquiring faith. Tennyson once said, "There is more faith in honest doubt, believe me, than in half the Creeds."

Here we don't care WHAT you believe, we only ask that you believe. Have some anchor, so that when the waves of alcoholic thinking start again to roll, you will be moored to something substantial enough to enable you to ride out the storm.

Looking back at our ambitions and aspirations we can recall many things we wanted and which we thought would make our lives complete. Some of them were impossible; they were the offspring of childish dreams, and later on, alcoholic wishing. Some of those things were possible for others but unattainable for us with our limited abilities.

We can now accept the fact that those things were not for us and wouldn't have been good for us if we had had them. Some of them we obtained and wished we hadn't. Their realizations were nothing compared to our expectations and the more we got the more we wanted. Ambitions were never realized because the more we advanced the more the horizons receded.

We are definitely what we think—as a man thinketh, so is he. The trick for all of us is to cull out of our thinking those thoughts that are injurious to us and to retain those that are beneficial.

We conceive our own thoughts, we give them birth, we nourish and sustain them—they are our brain children. Our lives become intertwined with them, and their influence on us and our behavior is enormous.

The thoughts we have must be purely conceived, carefully trained, well disciplined and encouraged. In so doing we surround ourselves with a group of brain children whose influence on our lives brings the happy results we can hopefully expect.

In our serenity prayer we accept with patience the things we cannot change in full knowledge that all emanates from God and is therefore Good, whether we recognize it as such or not. The courage to change the things we can, knowing full well that we are the instrumentalities through which God works. The knowledge to differentiate between the two is that to which we all aspire.

No longer can THINGS drive us to drink, for THINGS are something outside our being and can only enter our hearts and minds if we admit them. Our experience has taught us that our greatest misfortunes were frequently our ultimate good—even our years of drunken torture were a blessing in disguise, for only by this means would we have found our bigger and better way of life.

We admit that for US—whiskey is bad; but whether it is bad for someone else is simply a matter for them to decide.

We have no fight with alcohol itself, its brewers, distillers, distributors or retailers. We say its abuse is bad but we do not curse the darkness; rather we tend to positive, constructive efforts to help that individual who is groping in the darkness. For him we light a candle of Hope which becomes a beacon upon which he may set a new course to a peaceful harbor where the weary alcoholic may find peace and rest.

In AA we are truly only concerned with the internal and not the external qualities of the man. What you wear or fail to wear in the matter of clothes is of no consequence. If you are clean inside the outside eventually cleanses itself.

Evening gowns and tuxedos are all right for formal affairs but a well dressed heart and mind is for everyday wear and is a greater adornment than silks and jewels.

Remember just a short while back, when we took the miracles of the Bible with the proverbial grain of salt? They were to our way of thinking only parables, told in order to impress certain moral truths, or else they were the understandable inaccuracies of uneducated, highly superstitious people of those unenlightened days. We admitted the purpose of those stories was good but as for believing them—well, they were contrary to known scientific fact.

You who have been in AA only a short time, how many miracles contrary to scientific facts do you see about you? The halls of every AA meeting are filled with them. Miracles are not only possible—they are commonplace.

Like the philosophers of old, we are beginning to believe anything so long as it is incredible. We have seen enough of God to believe anything of Him.

Next to the God-inspired Program itself, we should be most thankful to our founders that they have resisted the pressure of various "movements" to ally themselves to us.

Reform movements are often only against something but AA is always FOR something. We do not resist evil but strive to overcome evil with good. Their forces are negative; ours positive.

Their machines stand idle while they strive to eliminate friction; ours run on power sufficient to overcome the friction, and the source of our power is infinite.

They say everything bad should be eliminated; we say everything bad is an opportunity, sent to us from God, that we may transform it to Good.

Nothing is impossible for God, therefore nothing is impossible for you and God if you are both playing on the same team. There is a big difference between being on God's team and getting God on your team.

To get on God's team we must train rigidly, know all the rules of the game, follow the instructions of the Great Captain in the spirit as well as in the letter, go to your Captain frequently when in doubt, co-operate with the other team members, do not try to be the big Star, be on the practice field early and stay late and put all you have into your efforts. Who knows—you might become a Regular upon whom God can rely to play his position as it should be played. One thing is sure—if you do make His team you are sure to win.

One of the first impressions of the non-alcoholic attending one of our meetings for the first time is the look of happiness upon the faces of our members. Time after time we have heard them comment on this fact. It is the characteristic that distinguishes us from the Dried-Up Drunks. The successful AA member radiates happiness as a natural consequence of his finding a new and happier way of living.

It is a revolutionary change for us belligerent drunks, but the cheerful face will materialize with our encouragement and as a result of our living the Program. Abraham Lincoln expressed this fact when he said, "Every man over forty is responsible for his face."

Faces are the windows through which we see the man.

The AA Program is so simple and so honest that it confounds the physician with his Latin prescriptions and the scientist with his intricate formulas. They have been looking for the answer through a microscope or a telescope while the solution was at their finger tips. No wonder AA astounds them—they have been like the old woman who tore her house down looking for her glasses, only to find them on her forehead.

The simplicity of our program is its attraction and we must keep it awfully simple or the results will be simply awful.

AA has had its remarkable growth not because of its affluence but because of its influence.

The eyes of the world are upon us for we stand out as the lone hope of a world driven to despair by alcohol.

Our every action is watched by those needing our program desperately. What will your influence be on them? Will you be a steppingstone or a stumbling block?

We alcoholics were up to our necks in the quicksand of yesterdays with a lifetime of tomorrows on our shoulders. Of course we sought escape in the bottle, for no man has courage and strength enough to survive this ordeal.

AA has taught us that TODAY is the only day we have. Those horrible TO-MORROWS which we hold in such dread have no substance except such as we give them in our living of successive TODAYS.

Yesterday is dead, tomorrow hasn't been, and may never be, born.

It is on the foundation of today that we build tomorrow.

We alcoholics are the world's greatest squanderers. During our drinking days we squandered our money, our health, our time, our intellect, our reputations, in fact everything—not for a purpose but to make ourselves oblivious to the fact that we were doing so.

We who have accepted the AA way of living must never give up our old habit but we should learn to spend ourselves for a constructive purpose.

That purpose is to help the other alcoholic. We are the best qualified people in the world for the job. Years of conditioning and thousands of dollars went into the process of making us experts. We have no other means of atoning for the past, no other way of showing our appreciation for the Grace of God which saved us, but to squander ourselves for this world-needed purpose.

Man was created in the image of God. We are told that the heart of man is the Temple of the Holy Ghost. A realization of this fact makes the desecration of the body as sacriligious as the desecration of any church.

We alcoholics have a lot of mess to clean up in our Temples in order to make them a fit place for communion with the God in us.

If we really want God to work in and through us in the rehabilitation of other alcoholics, we must provide Him at least a clean workshop.

On that awful day when the world had toppled about us, when all hope had departed and only wild desperation remained, then was the night darkest and nearest was the dawn. At this darkest hour we "hit our bottom." There was no way to go but UP.

As dawn follows darkness in Nature's scheme, so darkness follows again in its turn. All things, save God, are transitory and what one day can bring, another day can take away. Let us not feel too secure in our sobriety, for darkness will come in the regular course of events, and we must be sure we have provided ourselves with the Light which will enable us to keep our footing on the slippery paths ahead.

After several years on the Program, we still have to guard against rationalizing. When it comes to selling ourselves a bill of goods we are tops. Our drinking was most always occasioned by a "good reason," or so we thought; the real reason—the fact that we were alcoholics and therefore compulsive drinkers—never occurred to us. A good reason can always be found for our actions, but the real reason is frequently obscure. Lord, teach us to know the difference.

Nothing great was ever achieved without overcoming great obstacles and no hero of history deserves more acclaim than those who were triumphant over self.

But do not let us swell up too much with pride. If we are honest, we know that with our character-weakened souls, with our "fogbound" brains, we could accomplish nothing of ourselves. It was only when we, in our desperate surrender, threw our lives and our wills into His keeping that He, in His mercy, removed the obstacle.

Unknown, even to ourselves, there must have slept in us that Faith of a mustard seed, that can remove mountains.

To us alcoholics, our Twelve Steps of Recovery are the stars on which we set our course of sobriety. Like the seafaring man, we will not get them completely in our grasp, nor do we need to do so.

If we but follow the course they indicate, we too, will reach our haven.

Probably no class of people has been brought into deep and turbulent waters of life to the extent of us alcoholics. Thousands of us were saved by a merciful God and emerged from our ordeal cleaner and stronger. That we were spared can be attributed only to the Grace of God.

There is nothing haphazard about God's actions. He led us into deep water for a purpose; He extracted us for a purpose. Be sure you fulfill that purpose.

To shut off from our minds the re-collections of unpleasant yesterdays is of course impossible, but we can refuse to dwell on them unnecessarily, or to lash the present with the cruel whip of the past.

It was in the past that remorse, re-sentments and self-pity were found, but now we are doing our level best to lose them in order to insure a happy and sober present. Close the gate—we have passed through it.

In the hurry and press of our everyday living, too many of us fail to stop occasionally to allow our souls to catch up with us. We have no time to think upon those things which are of lasting value. We reserve our spiritual thinking for Sunday mornings and meeting nights, oblivious of the fact we must live every day. Find or make time this very day for just a minute with the Man Upstairs. Remember you need Him and He needs you.

Created in God's image, with the breath of God in my nostrils, my body the Temple of the Holy Ghost, called by the Christ a child of God, surely, I could walk with angels if I could only live up to my heritage.

Man has fallen short of his goal mostly because he has not thought he could do it. He timidly denies his own divine origin; he fails to credit the existence of God in him.

He is like the man who wants to fly but not so high that he can't keep one foot on the ground. His eyes are fixed on the skies but his feet are planted solidly on the earth.

We alcoholics were saved from un-numbered deaths in our drinking days and preserved for a purpose that only we could accomplish. God has His way of doing things and He selects people to be the instrumentality through which He works.

If you fail to fulfill your appointed function, then just that much of God's work goes undone until He finds another instrument through which to work.

You were not dragged from the gutter so that you might be able to enter your home and lounge before an open fire in ease. God saved you because He had work for you to do. Go do it.

You want the world to be better? Then be better yourself. True, you are only one individual in a thickly populated world, but your life touches hundreds of others and each of those touches hundreds more. Who knows how far the influence of one smile travels or where a word of wisdom will take root? Even should your influence for good extend no further than your own skin, there will be at least one less rogue in the world.

The difference between your pre-AA existence and your present is in direct ratio to the extent "God's way of living" has influenced your life.

Those of us who have witnessed the miracles in our own midst and who have felt the surge of power that we acquired when we tapped this unlimited reservoir, know that our "horsepower" is dependent on our God-power.

Many practicing alcoholics know their desperate need for AA, but are reluctant to do anything about it as they feel their friends would ridicule them, and so they continue drinking and making themselves ridiculous.

Too many of us put too much emphasis on the reactions of people whose reactions are not worth considering.

We should choose to want less of material things and more of substantial values.

Happiness comes not from possessions but from an ability to possess the things that assure happiness. Live up to the Twelve Steps as best you can and you will find your sense of values will change and that real, lasting happiness is within your reach.

AA is full of paradoxes. Our great Victory came as a result of our unconditional surrender; because we fell we are able to lift others; because of our mental, moral and spiritual illness we attained a health we never had in our non-alcoholic days; because we were social outcasts we have become the hope of society.

Alcoholism, which was our weakness, has indeed become our strength.

From the beginning of recorded history man has had his difficulties to overcome. In fact, history is a recording of these ordeals.

We, of this highly mechanized age, have turned our problems over to bigger and bigger machines to do our work for us. We have raised economic efficiencies to the point where we can provide all our needs and luxuries by easy work in just a few days a week. We are going soft.

No wonder, then, that when a problem confronts us we try to escape it by hiding in a bottle. We try to escape the seriousness of living, forgetting that when life ceases to be serious it will become a joke—at our expense.

No election is won or lost until all the votes are in. On that occasion when we felt all was lost, that we had utterly failed and despaired of help from any source, we found the doors of our Fellowship and learned the underlying causes of our failure.

It was the admission of our failure, our complete inability to manage our lives, that opened the door to the greatest blessing. Over and beyond sobriety, through happiness and peace of mind, we finally found a conscious contact with a God of our own understanding.

Comparatively early in our drinking careers we knew our principal fault was our drinking, and we even knew but would not admit that our other faults were the offspring of the first.

We changed brands, we switched from whisky to beer, we changed our drinking companions, we put more time between drinks, we changed jobs, wives, localities. Somehow it never occurred to us that the only way to deal with our drinking was to abandon it to a slow death by starvation.

You can't shoot, drown or strangle alcoholism but you can abandon it.

When we were drinking we all had an interest and it was all contained in the shortest word in the English language—I. Our conversations always started with—I need—I want—I said, etc. No wonder people crossed the street when they saw us coming. Our conversations were as obnoxious as our breath.

Take note of the older men on the Program; their conversations are seldom about themselves except as they fit into the other fellow's problems. It is no accident that they are popular with the group for they never bore you with themselves but instead they talk about your most popular subject—You.

Remember in Step Nine we were told to make direct amends wherever possible but this generous principle should extend further. We should endeavor to regulate our conduct so as never to intentionally hurt anyone.

Because we don't drink gives us no license to embarrass our host by telling the other guests what fools they are or what a great guy we are because we quit.

It gives us no right to hold our sobriety as a club over the head of friend wife and make her accede to our every whim on the threat that we will go out and hang one on.

AA gives no new liberties, only new responsibilities.

The sooner we alcoholics realize the fact that sobriety by itself is not enough to insure real living, the better off we will be.

For us to emerge from our shell and then cease all growth is to stagnate, and stagnation is death itself to an alcoholic. Everything on this planet has a part in the Grand Scheme and unless we discover and act our little part, we are dead, and decay has already set in.

It is contrary to the laws of Nature for man to stand still. We either go ahead or we go back.

The Program is often referred to as a Selfish Program and it is primarily that. Jesus of Nazareth told us to "Love our neighbors *AS* ourselves." We are supposed to love ourselves, and in so doing we should give to ourselves all the happiness we can. We have found out, however, by practical application, that we can only receive happiness if we give happiness.

We should fulfill all our duties to our families, to our communities, and to our neighbors so that we can keep in the good graces of our own conscience for that is the only avenue of approach to happiness and peace of mind.

If you really love that guy in the mirror, you must of necessity love your Creator and your neighbor.

The AA way of living holds out, for all that will grasp it, everything that is advantageous to life. A healthy mind, a healthy body, a healthy soul. Complete harmony with God, your fellow man and yourself. Truly the peace that passeth all understanding.

So many times we hear people say, "Don't preach to me about God. He has no time for the likes of me." It is hard for us alcoholics to conceive of a God, whom we have gone out of our way to alienate, who has time for the likes of us—yet we know that he does have time for us and has demonstrated this fact in hundreds of cases, just as though He had nothing else in the world to do.

The effectiveness of AA is largely built upon understanding and human sympathy. These characteristics were not acquired from a book but learned the hard way as we, too, traveled the long dark alley of despair in search of a helping hand and an understanding heart.

Creeds and ideologies are for preachers and students to debate and reason, but our doctrine of love and understanding has nothing to do with reason; frequently it is contrary to reason, as it comes from the heart and not the head

You cannot know and appreciate wisdom unless you are also acquainted with a liberal amount of pure folly. Folly provides the lessons that really stick in our memories and provide danger signals to govern our decisions in our future conduct.

For that reason the lessons learned overnight in a jail cell outlast those acquired after long periods of study. Believe you me, those lessons are seldom forgotten.

Criticism is often the sincerest form of flattery. We are all subject to it at times if we do anything at all. When criticism does arise, and before you build up a first rate resentment, think first—who is it that criticizes? What is the motive behind it? Is it constructive or just plain antagonistic? Is it prompted by jealousy or ignorance? Would you do the same thing again if you had it to do over? What does your conscience say about it?

No great man escaped having enemies; all the old masters had critics; all political and social reforms had their adversaries and the early disciples of all new religions were persecuted, stoned and crucified.

If you are criticized you may possibly be right, but if you are ignored you know you are wrong.

We alcoholics know that one drink is too much and a barrel isn't enough. That first drink starts the compulsion to drink.

Suppressing desires can become a habit just as their satisfaction does. Each time we say "NO" we weaken the old habit and strengthen the new.

The efforts to satisfy our desires led us to the excesses that brought about our alcoholism. So let us follow the advice of John Stuart Mill and "learn to seek our happiness by limiting our desires, rather than attempting to satisfy them."

Few of us who are successfully working the AA Program have failed to notice the almost immediate influence our sobriety has brought about, not only in our homes and jobs, but in the community as well.

Some of us who a short time ago stood before the judge and got the usual "ten dollars or ten days," are now frequently closeted in the Judge's Chambers at his invitation to assist him in his handling of the alcoholic problem.

We know what we were, we know what we are, now let us be what we can be.

Frequently we are asked "Why waste your money on that guy? He's a phony if ever I saw one." We have all heard this and often it was true but after all, the monetary loss each month was way below our old whisky bills. Every once in a while the long shot does come in and the pay-off is tremendous.

It is simply a case of betting on people instead of horses. These bets on people can't lose, for if the phony abuses your generosity, the fault is his, not yours and he is debited and you are credited by the Great Bookkeeper who has charge of the Treasury where "neither moth nor rust doth corrupt and where thieves do not break through and steal."

We know from past experiences that we actually invited all our troubles to enter our lives. We left the door wide open for them. Getting sober does not necessarily mean we have closed all the doors, for some of us have only closed the front door and left the back door wide open.

The chances are that you are not only vulnerable through the door marked Alcohol. As you advance to the front, watch well both flanks and the rear.

Many of us would have been ready to do something about our drinking problem years before we did, except for the obstinate determination not to allow the wife, mother or boss to tell us what to do.

In our drinking days our imagination fashioned fears of unknown tomorrows, resentments against those who wanted to help us most and a sense of failure, simply because we had no time to devote to succeeding; a compulsion to drink because we did not imagine we could live without drinking. We lived in a Hell of our own imagining, but we have found that we can transform that Hell into Heaven with this same medium.

The door of living that opened upon our advent into AA is also able to close upon those years of daily dying that are behind us. That door opened into a long hall that stretched out to a vanishing point; our eye could not perceive its end. We should not be content to just pass through this portal and close the door upon our past, but we should move on, for our happiness is up that hall, and we must constantly advance to attain our happy goal.

Life is too short even if we live the whole of it to its fullest, but we alcoholics have wasted so many years of our lives that we must now double our efforts if we hope to do any living at all. Truly, for us, it is later than we think.

There is one consolation, however, and that is, that it is possible to use a single moment to produce an eternity of benefits for humanity. Much time has been frittered away but there is still ample time to do good.

Life is not measured by its length but by its width and its depth.

In AA no man is the official mouth-piece of the Movement. No one person represents AA officially. Here you find a God of your own understanding; when you talk you give only your own opinions, you give your own interpretation to the Twelve Steps and practice them as you think they should be practiced.

If you use your method and stay sober, we will admit your way is good for you but we admit no authority on your part to tell us how to work them. Because it worked for you is no sign it might not be poison for someone else.

We have finally found a way to foil alcohol simply by refusing to look upon it as a beverage and rather as something to which we are allergic. We have found that we don't have to drink; we have demonstrated that we can be happier without it.

Now that we are sober, how are we going to use our sobriety?

Can we sit back and bask in this new-found sunshine? Forget it, kid. Better men than you have tried it. If still you don't believe it, go back to the gutter or the jail or the jitter-joint and ask those who tried that method.

One day we were practicing alcoholics, then in twenty-four hours we were on the Program — arrested cases.

Was it because one day we were weak and spineless and the next day we had completely reversed our character?

No, the Power had been there all the time but we had never before tapped it. Our best-intentioned friends had advised us to use our Will Power, not realizing that it was the stubbornness of our Will Power that made us persist in our drinking.

It takes a person of great will to continuously defy the pleas and threats of our combined worlds. No, it wasn't Will Power we lacked, it was Won't Power. We Won't take that first drink.

Few of us have any real direction to our conduct. We live from day to day, taking care of our problems as they arise, and this is sound AA advice as regards our long-range thinking and planning. This does not mean that we should take this too literally and give absolutely no thought to tomorrow's needs.

It is absolutely true that tomorrow may never be born, but, on the other hand, it might, and in that event a well filled refrigerator will come in mighty handy.

Do you hold some great resentment against anyone? Can you afford to keep it? Sure, I know he "done you wrong" but why? Was there any justification for it? Could you have been a little bit wrong also? Does everyone share your dislike for him? If they like him and you don't, how do you account for it? Is it possible they know him better than you do?

Catfish, as ugly as they are, make delicious chowder and a skunk has a valuable fur. No person is either entirely ugly or bad. Maybe there is something wrong with your vision or maybe you haven't gotten close enough to him to really see him.

So you have dried up — you're off the stuff. That's fine, but many of us have had to face the ridicule of our former drinking pals and unfortunately some of us couldn't take it.

Who was the ringleader of that jeering section? The chances are he was the guy who needed the program as badly as you did. He didn't want you sober because you were frequently worth the price of a bottle. He had no logical argument to use so he resorted to ridicule.

Remember that he who laughs at you tonight, tomorrow morning you can kid Hell out of.

When we become fully conscious that we, as men, are spirit primarily, that our bodies are but necessary instruments through which the spirit works; that the mind is not a collection of brain cells but is actually a series of thought waves as free of actual substance as the winds or the rays of light or heat, we appreciate the fact that chains are powerless to restrain the thoughts which are actually the mind.

We can and do select the thoughts we store up in these brain cells. We keep what we want and we discard what we please. The kind of thoughts we think become habit and so become us.

Man has taken the raw materials of Nature and created works of such beauty and power as to be second only to Nature itself, yet only an insignificant few have contributed materially in this work.

For the most part, man crawls through life on a plane but slightly higher than brute creation. The train of progress has a thousand deadheads for every paying passenger.

We are no longer bums but passengers on the train of progress who have not only paid our fare but are willing to get out and push when the going gets tough.

In our early days of sobriety, when our minds were still full of cobwebs, when we were unable to concentrate on what was being told us, when we were actually antagonistic to any spiritual help, many thousands of us were held on by the great bond of understanding, sympathy and friendliness of the Group.

We will dwell together in peace and harmony only so long as we are united in our one and only purpose of "carrying the message to other alcoholics."

We are organized for no other purpose, we have prospered in fulfilling that purpose, and we shall lose our sobriety and die as an organization when we depart from that purpose.

The mind of man is unable to approximate the untold millions of dollars that have been spent by us alcoholics in the futile chase after happiness, only to find that what we purchased was not happiness but misery, want, illness and despair.

By calling off the hunt, by quitting our quest for fun that we had always believed hid in the bottom of a bottle, we found happiness. The price of this happiness was only that we give happiness to others and we learned that the more we gave the more we had. We could eat our cake and have it too.

When God makes a tree it is exactly the species, size and shape He intended it to be. Nothing the tree can do will alter it in the slightest degree.

God, however, in His Wisdom, created man with all perfection, yet allows him to make of himself what he will. He gave us independent minds and wills because He intended that we, the highest form of all living beings, should work out our own mental and moral evolution from mortality to immortality.

It is very noticeable that most of the great religious teachers or prophets prescribed nothing but a code of morals and ethics. All their teachings were characterized by an almost complete lack of formal religious observances.

They have pointed out the direction but never the path. If we follow other men's paths we fall over the same stones they fell over and we got lost where they got lost. Each of us must carve out his own path and the progress we make will be determined by our own efforts to advance.

How many times have we postponed that call to the guy we sensed needed us? We felt that he didn't phone us just to "shoot the breeze." True, he didn't come right out and call for help, and we did have something else to do. We decided we would take care of it tomorrow and then found out that tomorrow was too late.

Today is truly the only day we have; what we can do, what we should do — we must do today.

The map of the United States is different today because Longstreet was one day late arriving at Gettysburg.

The dollar is worth but about half its value of only a few years ago. Capital gains taxes have depreciated all properties by twenty-five percent. Moneys invested in stocks and bonds can be swept away between dawn and dark. The sound investment of today can be a white elephant on your hands tomorrow.

Your dollars invested in the rehabilitation of human souls are the only investment that can't lose. The dividends are paid whether the project fails or not. This way you can't fail to win.

Too few people can distinguish the difference between the moderate or social drinker and the compulsive drinker. In fact, the line is so indistinct that the drinker himself does not know until it is too late.

The Niagara River is a smooth-flowing stream until it reaches the Falls and then, in a matter of feet, it becomes a churning torrent of danger and death.

Nothing in life is obtained except by pain and toil. This is sad news to us alcholics who have shunned both like smallpox most of our lives.

Let the famous musician tell you of his hours of dreary practice, the inventor of his hundred failures for each success, the boxing champ of his endless days of absorbing punishment in empty gymnasiums. Toil and suffering are a necessary prelude to success and we should bear our crosses, not as burdens, but as preparations for our ultimate victory.

No man ever lived without a God of some kind. If it was not the God of Abraham or of the Christian conception, it was the sun, or Nature or thunder or mythical gods. It was golden images or idols of wood, and to some it was money, or position or fame. We all had a God even if it was no more than a bottle.

No man, however brave, would have the temerity to face the forces of Nature and a hostile world unless he had recourse to something beyond his own puny strength.

Every time I hear an atheist sounding off I always think of the days when I denied the fact that I was an alcoholic, knowing, deep down inside, that I was kidding myself.

The only way that AA can be considered a Reform is in the fact that our way of living is the result of a reformation in our thinking.

Our new pattern of action is the result of a new pattern of thinking. As our thoughts are focused more and more on more and more, our minds grow in the capacity to absorb more and more.

As our thoughts are directed to the God of our understanding and our suffering alcoholic brethren we find that self is pushed back into the little space it deserves.

Jobs are as good or as bad as the mental attitude we have toward them. No man holds a job but what some other man is envious of him on its account and every job has its good and bad points.

Too often we hear the excuse that the job was the cause of the drinking, when most frequently it was the drinking that made the job obnoxious.

One man swinging a pick is digging a hole in the ground and his fellow workman besides him is doing his part in the erection of a Temple.

Maybe it's not the job at fault, maybe it's your attitude toward it.

We cannot give the new man our conception of the Program and expect him to get the same results as we. This is particularly true of the spiritual phases of our thinking. We must each seek and find our own solution, but we can tell him how we did it; we can direct his thinking along spiritual lines so that he too will find a God of his understanding and work out a system of procedure that will make the Program work for him.

To us alcoholics who were prone to give meanings to words that were not intended by the speaker, words are a particularly lethal weapon.

In our drinking days we invariably put the wrong interpretations on the best-intended words of our friends. We then sounded off with a flow of words that we did not mean and knew full well that we did not mean them. The thoughtless sentence or the fancied slight was forever coming between us and those we loved.

The world's attitude toward us, either friendly or hostile, is largely determined by our own words.

Life is not a succession of days on earth but rather it is an accumulation of experiences. Days are simply time locations where experiences transpired. The day on which no event occurred is a day lost out of life, for it had nothing in it to justify its memory.

No man with certainty can see beyond this instant. Yesterday we had a friend, hale, hearty and bubbling over with energy and ambition. Today we write a letter of condolence to his widow. No one knows the day or the hour but this we do know — we are alive right now, people are suffering right now, we can help them right now.

We in AA have many religious affili-
ations and there are some of us who
contend that AA is all the religion they
need. Yet this fact remains: the spiritual facts on which AA is based would
not have survived the ages but for the
tenacity of formal religions.

Without religions, our moral, political
and social structure would collapse.
There is a lot in all denominations that
can be criticized but without them life
would be chaos.

Many of us can recall being fired from jobs for drinking and at the same time being given a letter of recommendation that spoke in glowing terms about our ability. Of course the former boss was trying to be kind in avoiding any mention of the drinking problem, but such letters are actually dishonest, and it was equally dishonest when we used them to procure new jobs.

How much better it would have been if they had tried to do something constructive about the problem rather than lowering us in our own esteem by making us a party to the deceit.

Why is the world? Why are we here? What is our purpose? Why must we live and suffer and die? Without God there would be no answer. We do not know the great extent of God's purpose, but we do know that we as individuals, each and every one, must somehow fit into that purpose.

We can only know God as He has revealed Himself to us. We know His principal attribute is goodness. Therefore His purpose must be good and we can best serve that purpose by aspiring to the highest standard of goodness that we can conceive.

Do you want to be happy? Then go buy that strange kid on the corner a bag of candy. It may help cause his teeth to decay but what's a tooth between two glad hearts.

The truly great man can afford to be humble, for hundreds of others are exalting him. You have only one horn to blow and other people can't toot it if you are eternally tooting it yourself.

The proud man is aggressive in his own interest; the humble man is aggressive in the ideals he believes in. Humility is not passive resignation; it is rather, subjecting self for lofty purposes.

We as alcoholics are so used to getting by with a minimum of effort on our part that we sometimes fail to appreciate that only those things earned have any real and lasting value.

We allowed our families to cover up for us and support us, we panhandled, we were experts in the game of something for nothing.

Nothing free is worth having. AA has no initiation fees or dues but it also costs a lot if you want to get a lot. You can procure a two-bit brand of AA but we don't guarantee it will work.

What exists in the life to come we can leave to the theologians, but the actual existence of Heaven and Hell here on earth is indisputable to us who have lived in both.

If most of the Bible thumpers that continually rave about the threats of Hell could know the Hell the poor practicing alcoholic is going through, it would scare them to death.

Reduced to its simplest form, the only true worship is to love God, and the only way to demonstrate this love is to serve your fellow man.

We in AA show the extent of our moral growth in the extent of our service to others. It is the only true spiritual experience. The flash of light that some of us experience could be only the first ray of intelligence that finally penetrated the alcoholic fog and dazzled our minds.

The true spiritual experience is evidenced by a passion to do those things which delight the spirit. By their works shall ye know them.

In the beginning, God created the heavens and the earth and all things therein contained. There is nothing on earth that God didn't put here.

True, we have manufactured things by changing sizes, shapes or chemical combinations but all things made by man can be reduced to those elements that God originally put here on earth. All things therefore are God's and he put them here for our use. He did not intend that we should hoard up surpluses and thus deprive others of their use.

Our responsibility begins in our use of these surpluses. It's God's not ours, remember? And some of God's loved ones are in want.

It was very hard for us alcoholics to realize that God has a big world on His hands and that He has other chores than just to give us rain when we want rain and sunshine when we want sunshine. We always thought the Universe revolved around us.

That He knows His job is evidenced by the regular return of days and seasons, by His distribution of weather in such a manner that the world has never been devoid of food. Think what chaos would exist if He had allowed us to run it our way.

God has given us many controls over Nature, but He knows the limits of human intelligence and the extent of human selfishness.

You can eat yourself to death as quickly as you can drink yourself to death. Working unreasonable overtime will bring on extreme fatigue that you may think "necessitates" a stimulant.

Too much zeal is fanaticism and Twelve Stepping without due regard to your own welfare can land you in trouble up to your neck.

Easy does it.

Can you imagine a state of mind absolutely free of fear? It is extremely hard for us who have had Fear, Worry and Uncertainty as constant companions most of our lives. To attain such a state of mind is only possible where there is complete Faith in God. Somehow, too, it would appear that it would mean complete faith in our fellow man and in ourselves.

Maybe this is too much to expect but you can try to cultivate more faith day by day and as you do, you will find more and more peace of mind and less and less of worry, fear and uncertainty. It works.

Many of us, when we get over the Big Trouble, whisky, sit back complacently and begin to enjoy our sobriety.

To work the Program successfully, we must remember "First Things First" and also remember that whisky is only the first. There are many other conflicts ahead and we must press on to successive victories over our many character defects to achieve a new way of living.

The conflict will never end until you arrive at perfection, or still more probably, the grave.

When you begin to rest complacently on your oars, you will find your boat is drifting downstream.

Look back, my friend, on the interminable nights of sweating, shaking, pacing the floor, praying for the dawn, yet dreading what the day would bring. That stretch in the "can" when "every day was like a year, a year whose days were long." Days that lasted a lifetime and nights that lasted an eternity.

Those days and nights are gone, through the Grace of God, and now there are not enough hours in each day, not enough nights in each week and the span of life seems insufficient to accomplish the goals we have set for ourselves.

Many Groups and Clubs permit a little "friendly game" in the clubrooms. Far be it from us to criticize anyone for anything, as we like a little game occasionally ourselves, but we have all known of cases where the games got out of control. We have well deserved reputations for intemperance.

Card games can be the breeding place for a grand emotional upset and, incidentally, it does not help a fellow's chances of sobriety to send him home broke to the wife and kids.

When the wife would take me to task in my drinking days, I would soon show her who was boss of the establishment. I would tell her in no uncertain terms that "When I ceased being Captain of the ship, I would sink it."

Oh, yes, I was Captain but somehow the ship was continually on the rocks. It wasn't my fault, understand, the wind and the waves were always against me.

Now I have resigned my commission as Captain, I have a new Navigator and my ship keeps pretty well on its course. I'm only a deck hand now but I'm happier with less responsibility and I am confident it's much safer.

We alcoholics have learned that if we fight liquor we are bound to lose. We always have. Our only hope is a complete abandonment of any ideas that we might have once entertained that we can drink. We must get sober and learn to like it. We should throw ourselves into all group activities, make our friends from the membership, read all AA literature and other spiritually inspiring books we can get, brush up on our praying.

As you practice this you will find that whisky will get further and further from your minds and when you do think of it you will regard it as a beverage for some guys, but poison for yourself.

When we alcoholics arrived at that point in our drinking careers that we commonly call "our bottom"; when difficulties were pouring in from every side; when there was no longer any room left to retreat and all our defenses had crumbled — we found that we had no other alternative but take the last desperate effort of the totally beaten.

AA proved, as history has often done, that the best defense is a strong offense.

Many persons look upon AA as something new and revolutionary whereas it is just the reverse. We have no new thoughts or doctrines and we have certainly discovered no new cures.

Our medications are those administered two thousand years ago. Our philosophies were borrowed, not word for word but in substance, from the Great Book our mothers read to us as children.

While science experimented for new and certain cures, we dug out the old but still potent prescription and administered it with sympathy and understanding. We can attest to the fact that it still works.

In Step Eight we "made a list of all persons we had harmed and became willing to make amends to them all."

It is a lot easier to list those persons whom we have harmed by some intentional and direct action than it is to list those whom we have hurt by acts of omission.

We have not only done those things which we ought not to have done, but we have left undone those things which we ought to have done.

Carelessness, neglect, lack of appreciation, and thoughtlessness can hurt as much as a kick in the teeth.

Men may call themselves atheists, agnostics, unbelievers, or what have you, but the fact still remains that man must believe in something.

If he thinks his own presence here on earth is simply an accident in the forces of nature, then he must believe that the forces of nature are able to create him with all his delicately adjusted organism. To do this the forces of nature would need to have intelligence in a very high degree and in addition there must be a tremendous creative force to carry out the dictates of that intelligence. He, himself, could not do this so this force of nature is superior in a vast degree to himself. Bingo! he has found the God of his understanding, let him call Him what he may.

Man is the only animal that smiles and he is the only one that has need of it. Not that God provided more for the animal kingdom than He did for us, but man, through the stupid misuse of his will power and his other advantages, has brought misfortunes upon himself that would be unendurable but for the healing balm of smiles and a sense of humor.

No man is completely beaten as long as he can smile, and we know from past experience that we can wade out of most of our messes on the stepping stones of good humored grins.

Loneliness drives more people to the Gin Mill than almost any other single factor — perhaps even the compulsion to drink.

In the old days when our society was objectionable to all our old friends, we would from sheer boredom go to the bar just to talk to someone. Anyone's conversation was preferable to our thoughts. The drink was frequently only incidental.

Boredom is still one of our worst enemies. If you have an AA club, there is always some guy you can try to help. Regardless of your effect on him, the experience is bound to help you and will relieve you of your blues.

It has always been a source of amusement to observe how belligerent people get in religious controversies and it is usually true that the less religion they practice the more they are prone to argue about it.

A convert is anyone who deserts some other form of religion and accepts yours or mine, while a renegade is one who deserts either yours or mine. Your convert may be my renegade.

Those who have the real spirit of the Golden Rule don't have to fight over religion for they have it, they know they have it and they know no one can take it from them.

All things in life are relative. Without night there would be no day; without evil there would be no good; without sorrow there would be no joy.

Drunk or sober, clouds will occasionally appear on the horizon but most of them will blow away. Storm will sometimes break upon us but if we are prepared we can ride it out and the rainbow will follow giving promise of better things ahead.

Yesterday's rain enhances our pleasure in today's sunshine.

Your Area Headquarters can probably use some additional help on the desk or perhaps a receptionist to interview new people calling at the club for help. They probably have a pressing need for Twelve Steppers or people who have a car and are available a day a week. Maybe they could use some speakers or even chair setter-uppers.

How about your Group? It takes people to distribute and collect ash trays. It's possible you might come in handy preparing or distributing refreshments.

Whatever your talents are it is a safe bet they can use you. Then the Group will become Your Group. Don't wait to be drafted — Volunteer.

The churches in their quarrels over purely sectarian issues have done much to divert attention from the primary purpose of religion, which is spirituality.

Some pastors take a more critical attitude toward the neglect of church duties than they do toward moral transgressions.

AA should be kept free of all controversial questions. We have but one purpose and that is to help the suffering alcoholic. Ours is a way of life; not a way of worship.

When we take the first drink we invite the dead certainty of physical illness, untold sorrows, shame and degradation. That first drink has built more hospitals, jails, poorhouses and insane asylums than any other cause. All the drinks that follow are simply compounding the felony.

There are some people that can drink intelligently, but these people avoid difficulties. We are not in that class and experience has proven it. Years of sobriety will not enable us to join that class, and again, experience has proven it. Why do you persist in trying, what are you trying to prove? That you are the exception to the rule? If you are the exception you automatically become a freak.

It would be possible for a nation, or even the world, to exist without many of the natural resources we have, but no nation could exist wtihout men. The strength of the nation is the strength of its men.

The men who comprise the population of the nation are individuals and the sum total of the virtues of the individuals is the character of the nation.

Our value to society is not our new-found sobriety but our new character as developed by our new and better way of living.

The reasoning of the practicing alcoholic is in such foul shape that he is apt to take any attitude on the drinking question and usually does.

It is unreasonable to expect them to view their own or anyone else's sobriety in a rational way. Naturally plain common sense is not possible in the midst of an alcoholic fog, but why — oh, why do so many practicing alcoholics, including slipees, invariably persist in looking for the most insecure member of AA in their quest for a drinking partner?

If you are homesick for the gutter, go on back to it, but don't take anyone with you.

Man is a pretty smart duck, but after all these centuries of study, experimentation and reasoning, we still don't know what we are, where our life came from, or what happens to it when we die. True we have certain faiths and beliefs, but who can say with certainty and with personal knowledge, exactly what the answer to the Great Enigma really is?

We have unlocked many of the secrets of Nature but we still don't know what we are, how we got here or where we will go when we leave.

God still has many secrets. If man knew them all there would be no incentive to know God better.

Many of us came into AA either in middle life or beyond and feel that with our reasonable life expectancy, it is practically impossible to atone for our previous wrong actions. The thief at the crucifixion probably thought the same thing, but by one single act he brought the promise that "this day thou shalt be with me in Paradise."

Real reforms are in people, not in movements. All the laws and demands of church, state and family could not make us change our drinking habits, but the day eventually came when we wanted to change, and then, and then only, was the change possible. Prohibition legislation was only a challenge to us and we drank the more because they said we could not. We were determined to show those So-and-Sos they couldn't stop us.

Only when we, ourselves, wanted to do something about it was any real reformation possible.

The span of human life is such a small part of eternity that the length of your life, whether it be twenty years or a hundred, is of no moment. Yet the life span of some men has, and will continue to have, great influence upon many succeeding generations.

If you can by one single act do something that will benefit just one person fifty years from now, you will have done more than millions who have gone before you. Few leave anything to posterity when they die that will outlive their tombstone.

Effort has been made to carry AA into schools and young people's organizations, but the effective response has been so negligible that it has usually been abandoned after a short trial.

AA is a program for ALCOHOLICS — persons suffering from alcoholism. It was designed to appeal to them and them only. It is probably true that we can tell the kids a lot about drinking, but it will fall on deaf ears. Unfortunately, we must be pricked by the sharp thorn of experience in order to learn.

It is most discouraging to many of us to find, after many weary months of trying to work on our moral inventory and studied efforts to eliminate some of our worst character defects, that the more we do the more we find to do. It is not that we are not making progress but as we study ourselves from a coldly analytical viewpoint, we find more defects than we ever realized we possessed.

Do not become discouraged when this situation exists. It is very evident proof of progress that you have come to a conscious realization that these new defects exist and you are at least bringing them out in the open where you can get a crack at them.

The aim of AA is not Sobriety but Happy Sobriety. The most effective and incidentally the soberest group, is the happiest group. It is possible that you can't speak at meetings, maybe you are not in a position to "carry the message," but you can and should show your happy sobriety in the radiance of your smile. It is our only advertisement and it should outshine in brilliance the gaudiest of neon signs.

The poor guy still in the gutter isn't interested in your sobriety, he's interested in the price of another drink. He is, however, very much interested in happiness. It's what he has been looking for all his life and thought he could buy by the "fifth."

The United Nations and the old
League of Nations both recognized the
fact that man's conquest of time and
space has brought the nations of the
earth into such close and intimate relationship that national problems are now
world problems and must be dealt with
accordingly.

Their lack of success, up to the present time, stems from their inability to
recognize the common Fatherhood of
God and the inherent brotherhood of
man. They attempt to settle world affairs without consulting the Power that
made both the world and the men in it.

George Washington is often credited with being America's first millionaire, yet few people are aware of this fact. He left a heritage so much richer politically, economically and historically, that his own personal wealth is forgotten.

His personal wealth has long since been dissipated but the opportunities in this country he helped establish, will continue as long as men's lives are motivated by the same unselfish devotion to mankind that he exemplified, both in public and private life.

The reformed drunkard has simply corrected his former drinking abuses. With this single exception he is the same man with the same defects of character that marked his life in his drinking days.

In contrast, the real AA has experienced a revolutionary moral change. He has put the operation of his life into the care and under the direction of the God of his understanding. Not only has he corrected his drinking abuses but he has turned his entire life over to the care of Him who is the source of, and indeed is, Good.

When we emerge from under our tons of troubles, get back on our feet and begin to live like other folks again, we somehow feel that the world has become a better place and that when our troubles vanished, all troubles vanished and there were few, if any, left in the world.

The store of world troubles is as great now as ever — only different people are having them. If you have no troubles of your own, go out and find somebody else's. They are not half so hard to carry and your heart and soul need the exercise.

AA is the outgrowth of a long period of experimentation. It is true that two men conceived the idea but it was only incorporated into a working plan after pooling the experiences of a hundred more.

The "Big Book" is a collection of ideas and experiences. There is no one in AA who can say "I, and I alone, conceived the idea in its entirety, I, and I alone organized it; I, and I alone control it." No man — with all due appreciation to the founders — developed AA, for AA is a program of growth; it has grown from the day of its inception and is still in the process of growth and development.

We move onward and upward, side by side and hand in hand, helping and sustaining one another. This way we will advance, but when someone begins to control and command, deserters will outnumber recruits.

We often wonder at the co-operation given us by non-alcoholics wherever AA takes root. A lot of it probably results from a high sense of public spirit; some lend their support because they have no valid reason for opposition; some because of admiration of the fact that we are one organization that hasn't got its hand out continually.

We strongly suspect though, that most of it is due to the fact that the alcoholics, the near alcoholics and the potential alcoholics represent a pretty fair majority of any community.

We have to think our way out of the quagmire we drank ourselves into. No one led us there and no one can lead us out. The older members can give you a few clues or hints but in the final analysis you have to figure it out for yourself in order to get permanent results.

You will find as you travel up that long road alone, however, that you have a host of real friends on the sidelines to cheer you on your way.

God has done some mighty fine work with what the world thought was very indifferent material. St. Paul and St. Augustine were two examples of men that God chose that no personnel officer in the world today would have given the OK. AA is full of similar examples where God has chosen the godless and made him His instrument for the performance of good work.

The tremendous energy, zeal, initiative, enthusiasm, and ambition that were factors in our becoming alcoholics, now diverted to better use, make us well qualified to serve in God's cause.

The life of any individual is a wonderful book; it is a love story; one of adventure and travel. It is biography and it is poetry. It is spiritual and it is tragic. It is everything rolled into one, for it is life, and life is every human emotion and experience.

The story does not end until the last line of the last chapter is completed. God is the author and He records a true portrayal of the character of the actors in the story, and the book will end "happy-ever-after" only if we, the actors, live our roles as He directed.

God will help only those who honestly try to help themselves. We in AA know the truth of this statement for it was only when we, by a definite act on our part, determined to do something about our drinking that God made available that Power that enables us to recover our sanity.

If your house is on fire it is very well to pray but the prayers will avail little unless you are running for a hose while you are praying.

The medical profession is sincere in its efforts to help the alcoholic. Unfortunately, however, the very nature of the ailment defies adequate diagnosis, as the causes cannot be localized or catalogued. Every alcoholic is a sick man, but the underlying cause of his sickness cannot be X-rayed because there is no one underlying cause. It is a progressive disease and the patient himself does not know where the pain really is.

We in AA, however, know our patient as we know ourselves, for drunks are strangely alike fundamentally. We know the symptoms and the effects of the malady for we too have suffered it. We know our medicine for its relief, for we were cured by it ourselves.

Alcoholism may develop from any number of hidden causes. We may be very much un-alike in our behavior when drinking but in the hang-over stage we are as alike as two peas in a pod. We know what to do in a case like that.

Life is to a very great extent a matter of choice. It is true we do not choose our parents, our birthdays or the day on which we die but that is about all.

It therefore follows we are largely what we choose to be. We made a very radical change in our lives when we chose not to drink and what further gains we make in life will be, likewise, of our own choosing.

So many times we have seen the practicing alcoholic helped over a period of months and even years, and each time someone labored over him they were rewarded by failure after failure. Surely the Twelve Stepper had done his very best. It was apparent that this guy just didn't want it or he was so far down the ladder he couldn't be helped.

Intelligence or common sense would say, drop him flat, yet there is hardly a group today that does not number among its regulars one or more people of this type. These men owe their present sobriety to the fact their sponsors had more heart than brains.

There is such an abundance of religions, sects, creeds and cults, that it is little wonder that many thousands of non-alcoholics have thrown up their hands in disgust and proceeded to ignore them all. The poor confused alcoholic certainly could not be expected to wade through this maze of contradictions.

To them the simplicity of the AA program has been its greatest attraction. Here they have been asked only to seek a God of their own understanding and to accept a spirituality based on common sense and universally accepted moral standards.

Is revenge really sweet? Some louse has offended you, so you get even, thus offending him and becoming a louse yourself.

Do you really want revenge? Then do the guy a favor. It will hurt him deep down in his heart as nothing else can. It will be a great source of satisfaction to your wounded pride and it may be that you will be additionally rewarded by the acquisition of a friend.

Our great triumph was not because of our victory over alcohol but because of our complete defeat. It was only when we were beaten to our knees that we sought the only help that could save us. So we came into AA, not as boastful conquerers but as cringing and bloody casualties of an unequal fight. We were whipped; we knew it; we gave not a damn who else knew it. For us it was unconditional surrender. There were and could be no reservations.

Think back to those days when we would creep off to our dens where we were holed up, and there like animals try to satisfy our appetites alone — so horribly alone. Just drinking, drink after drink, and dying slowly of despair. If we had a friend in the world we didn't know it. We just wanted to drink and die alone.

It was people who brought us out of this pit, people of marvelous sympathy and understanding, and now, joining hands with these people, we have learned the joy of living — not alone, but with, and a part of a community of people.

Until man looks upon the face of God, he cannot, with his limited faculties, know God. We can and do know some of His attributes as He has disclosed them to us in the world.

We can, however, study ourselves. We can cultivate those good qualities we discern and we can eradicate the bad. We do know many of the attributes of God and we can emulate them. We can aspire to Godlike virtues and if we then do not know God, perhaps God will know us.

Our lives today are a series of compromises. Legislators enact laws which are compromises to both contending factions. Juries bring in verdicts which they don't even profess to be in accordance with the law and the evidence, and excuse their verdicts on the ground that it was a necessary compromise. Even the religions of the day are frequently adjusting their codes of do's and don'ts in order to effect a compromise with their more liberal elements. Our national and international relations are based upon political expediency rather than sound political principles of justice.

Where moral principles are involved there is no such thing as compromise — it must be either morally right or morally wrong.

If we deny the fatherhood of God and our divine relationship to Him and each other, then we are but animated pieces of clay, each one independent of and unconnected with each other. If that be so, then we are foolish to love and labor for others. But are love and charity nonsense? Would life be a pleasant and interesting experience without them? No, if we removed these characteristics from our lives we would be left with only that which the baser animals possess.

We veterans of the Alcoholic Wars that raged within ourselves can bear testimony to the fact that it was only when we called upon the God of our understanding, that peace was restored to our lives.

World Wars are but the extension of the conflicts existing in the souls of men on a world-wide basis. They, too, have as their foundation, fear, suspicion, envy, intolerance and national egotism.

There will never be a permanent peace until the Prince of Peace is admitted into the hearts of men in high places and is allowed to preside over their Conference Tables.

"God created the world and God saw everything He had made, and behold, it was very good." He gave man dominion over the world and we have badly fouled it up.

This world, with all its wars, crimes, sins and sorrows, is truly our world — not the one God made.

Alcoholics and non-alcoholics alike must get out of the driver's seat, admit we are powerless over our baser instincts and let God take over.

Then our world will become His world again and it will be very good indeed.

The only impossible thing in the world is a full conception of the things that are possible.

Within the limits of our lifetime we have seen many marvels; the transmission of sound and pictures across the continent without visible means; we cook and freeze with the same unit of energy; man can now exert a force of twenty thousand tons simply by pushing a button. Nothing seems beyond the vision of the scientist in his study and use of the unlimited forces of Nature.

The power of God, however, is still virgin territory. Man hasn't scratched the surface in his efforts to put this force to work for man. When this is accomplished the word "impossible" will not be in anybody's dictionary.

Our cute little darling and that spoiled brat across the street do exactly the same tricks.

Man is so constructed that he cannot be absolutely impartial. It is contrary to human nature.

We can, however, pause and reflect before we pass judgment, and we can try to put ourselves in the other fellow's position. We are prone to judge him solely on his acts while we judge our acts by our motives and thus excuse ourselves.

Doubt is the opposite of Faith. No man has either one completely, but even those of little faith have by far more faith than doubt. He may not admit a belief in God or the inherent good in mankind but still there are numberless things in which he has no doubt.

If he did not have some faith he would be afraid to go to sleep for fear he wouldn't waken; he would refuse to eat a meal unless he cooked it himself. He would be afraid to leave his wife to go to work or to leave his job to return to his wife for fear they would not be there when he returned.

Reduced to its simplest form, life is good or bad in proportion to our faith and our doubts.

To follow the letter of the law is not enough. You can be moral without difficulty in "solitary."

Do not let your morality be simply restraining and abstaining. Be constructive in your goodness. Be good for something.

Love is as necessary to a human being as sunshine is to a plant. Without it the soul of man withers, shrivels and dies. Fortunate is the man who has love given to him but even more fortunate is he who earns it. The only way to earn love is to love. Thou shalt love thy God with all thy heart and thy neighbor as thyself.

He who hoards love shall lose it, but he who scatters love about him as he moves through life finds that it takes root and surrounds him on every side.

Life has been hard on us but most of it was made hard by ourselves. The hard life, however, taught us much; it strengthened our muscles; it broadened our experiences. We are better men because of it. We have known much of hunger, pain, defeat, mental anguish, despair and shame. Only the good survived this ordeal and we can alleviate the sufferings of the world all the better because we have suffered also.

God was not punishing us . . . He was conditioning us.

We are all familiar with that class of people who have a drinking problem; they know they have it and they know that they can do nothing about it themselves. They also know that we had a similar problem and that we did something about it; their own eyes bear testimony to that effect —yet they refuse to take the message we bring them. They have ears yet they will not hear. It is not our purpose to sell them a bill of goods. Our message is only for those who want it. They aren't ready yet, so conserve your efforts for those who are hungry for what we have to give.

For a person to attempt to live apart from this world is as useless as for a drop of water to live apart from the ocean. God put everything in this world and He takes nothing out. To endeavor to withdraw from the world's activities is another way of fooling yourself. We are an influence for good or evil regardless of our attempts to hide from society at large.

When a rock falls from a cliff into the sea, it is not merely that the land is one rock less, it means the contour of the whole continent has changed. However, it is still a part of God's Universe whether it can be seen by man or not.

Each of us has only so many hours to live and we alcoholics have wasted far too many of them in the past.

New men, by the thousands, are crowding our doors, searching for our Message of Hope. Those who are endeavoring to carry the Message are frequently pushed to the limit of their available time for this purpose.

Have you the right to monopolize the time of the Twelve Steppers by indulging yourself in so-called slips?

We come into AA and are told that we should endeavor to establish a conscious contact with our God as we understand Him; that we should, through prayer and meditation, get on speaking terms wtih Him. We brushed up on our rusty salutations of "Almighty" and practiced on our Thees and Thous only to learn that there was a simpler and more direct approach.

We found that we could "tune God in" to our hearts and consciences and that no other method was needed to send and receive messages. We learned that what we said was of no great consequence anyway, as our prayers were for His will, not ours, and we also learned that we had to make no direct request for those things that were for our good, as He knew our needs before we ever realized them ourselves.

The harvest is great and the laborers are too few. Too often we get a new man, we work diligently on him, get him to a meeting or two and then another new man appears and we drop the first one and frequently never see him again.

This is not to imply that we are to carry him on our backs indefinitely, but we can utilize an occasional spare ten minutes to call him on the phone. We can keep our eyes open for him at the meetings and if he misses several in succession, we can look him up.

Remember you were the midwife at his rebirth in this new life and you should not neglect him in his AA infancy.

A split second separates the past, the present and the future. The course of history has been altered in a moment of decision on the part of one man. Inventions that have revolutionized our mode of living may have taken years to perfect but the idea behind them was born in a flash of thought between the ticks of a clock.

In that great day when you determined that you had had enough, that you were whipped, the resolve took but a fraction of a second, but in that instant you closed your past and opened your future.

A moment of thoughtlessness can put you back in the past again.

Alcoholics are by nature the great "I AM." We work ourselves into a lather in doing AA work and sometimes we are rewarded with a degree of success and we begin to puff up like a pouter pigeon, forgetting we are of ourselves able to do nothing. We are still but a drink away from a stumble-bum.

We are what we are by the Grace of God only. We accomplish what little we do by a Power greater than ourselves. How can you help anybody? You were never even able to help yourself.

Before the philosophy or theory of AA was ever committed to writing the "Big Book", it was devised by the Founders after many trials and errors, after many disheartening failures and setbacks.

Because of our phenomenal growth we are prone to think our birth was painless.

AA was not invented; it was born in the labors of suffering men and women, who, by pooling their common experiences, arrived at an answer to the alcoholic problem—one that would work.

In our drinking days most of us entertained frequent ideas about suicide, but we did nothing about it because we either lacked the nerve, lost our ability to make and carry through any decision, or we still had some hope that sometime, somehow, something could be done. We were still in love with life, rotten as our living was.

The real joy of living came only when our living had some purpose and it will stay sweet as long as we actively engage in constructive, purposeful living.

Opportunity is found within ourselves and nowhere else; the place that provides the greatest opportunity for our mental, moral and physical welfare. Only when we are mentally and physically fit are we able to recognize and grasp material opportunities when they present themselves. Billion dollar deals have been cooked up in practically every bar in the country but they have all vanished into thin air during the following morning hang-over.

Our reason is the creator of all our conditions of life, whether they be legitimate or illegitimate. We think ourselves into stormy and turbulent living just as surely as we think ourselves into peace and serenity.

Our stinking drinking was as much a product of our stinking thinking as was our stinking thinking the result of our stinking drinking.

The man who has the greatest trouble in getting our program is frequently the man who is above the average in education. He tries to open the door to our philosophy of living with his Phi Beta Kappa key. It just won't fit.

The man who enters our door convinced that all he knows hasn't been enough to keep him out of difficulty, who is willing to unlearn all those things he knows that are not so, and who, in humility, is willing to open his mind and heart to the simple wisdom of those who have succeeded where he has failed, is almost a sure bet.

Don't kid yourself, pal. You want to drink but you can't. You never can. Admit it. Accept it — then forget it.

You can get sobriety — so get it, keep it and like it.

It's as simple as that.

If we mean it when we say "Thy will be done," then what God wills is what we will. Happy and sober will be the man or woman who acquires this frame of mind.

If you want all your prayers answered your way, then let your way be God's way.

Too frequently we get God and Santa Claus mixed up.

It takes very much more skill to erect a house than it does to tear one down. Jesus of Nazareth could be crucified but His teachings could not be killed. His influence today exceeds that of all the Caesars, the Hannibals, the Napoleons and the Alexanders rolled into one.

These elementary truths were taught in differing forms by other religious teachers before and after His time. The principles of the Golden Rule are as old as civilization, for it is the very basis of civilization.

By the grace of God, we alcoholics have acquired certain characteristics that have made us beneficial to the earth. We have become in fact the salt of the earth.

If, however, we hoard our savour to ourselves and fail to recognize our responsibility to distribute it to those portions of the earth that need it, then have we indeed lost our savour and it is good for nothing but to be cast out and to be trodden underfoot of men.

Nothing is a blessing unless we put it to some constructive use. The wealth of the world is useless to a starving man on an uninhabited and barren island.

Out in the world we brush elbows with men, but in solitude we learn intimately about God and ourselves. Great truths are only born in solitary thought, never in crowded auditoriums.

God has some work to be done that only you can do. You have some problems that only He can solve. Why not sit down together sometime, just you two, and talk it over.

We alcoholics are in all things extremists. We either overindulge or we must abstain entirely. Drinking is not the only field however, where this characteristic is noticeable — it exists even in the way we practice our AA.

Many of us who thought nothing of paying ten or even twenty dollars a quart for liquor in Prohibition days, feel that we are more than generous when we drop a quarter in the basket on meeting nights.

Probably if we all loosened up a little more, our Committees would be able to do those things that we now criticize them for not doing.

A cheap brand of AA is no bargain.

We alcoholics are obstinate people. We drank all the more because people told us we couldn't; when they said we were drunken sots and were hopeless — then we quit.

Man's relationship to the mule is very close.

Your life, like mine, has probably been a long series of wrongs committed against you. They probably number a thousand or more. How many still bother you? Only those you still remember. For your own happiness and peace of mind, forget them.

If you were asked to give a definition of the AA Program, you could probably come no closer than to say it is a Thinking Program.

Underlying the whole philosophy is a studied effort to change the mental fumbling of the alcoholic to real, profound, constructive thinking.

It was this type of thinking that inspired our movement, and because of the profound thought behind it, it developed the simplicity that makes it understandable to the befogged alcoholic and yet so profound as to confound the wise.

Centuries ago a man learned to ignite wood artificially. No one in the world today knows his name, but all modern inventions are directly or indirectly traceable to his act. What his name is doesn't matter but every skyscraper in the world is his monument. His name perished as all names are apt to do, but his almost juvenile act of starting fire by friction will live as long as civilization does.

A single word you utter might kindle a fire that would burn through the ages.

We alcoholics have lived in two entirely different worlds that were separated only by an act of decision.

One day we lived in a world filled with hostile people, a world devoid of understanding and sympathy; a world of ugliness, suffering and despair. By this act of decision, a new day was created and we were transported into a different world.

If you would change the world, change yourself.

Many members of AA refer to their entrance into our fellowship as a passing from adolescence to maturity. When we take this step we should cease thinking as children and begin to think as adults.

Remember how you wanted what you wanted when you wanted it, and cried like hell when you didn't get it? The advice of wiser and saner folks fell on deaf ears and we persisted in having our way even though our way was killing us.

A child thinks with its appetites while a mature person thinks with his head. We all know what class we belonged in.

Drunkenness is unthinkable for a thinking person.

It takes courage, intelligence, initiative and deep emotions to make a really successful fool. The timid, underimaginative. cowardly seldom do.

We as alcoholics made fools of ourselves, it is true, but, in so doing, we experienced more, we lived more, we suffered more. These are the ingredients of a liberal education.

If wisdom could be dissected, there would be a large portion of Folly, Defeat, Suffering and just plain Damned Foolishness in its make-up.

By the same token, our foolishness taught us valuable lessons that could not have been acquired anywhere else.

The poor old drunk has ever had to face the wrath of the law and an indignant world. Lectures, threats, jail sentences, booby hatches and asylums have proven to be but waste of words, efforts and public funds. Nothing — absolutely nothing worked.

AA tried a revolutionary ministration of sympathy and understanding. It recognized his condition as an illness, threefold in its nature, and that the only medication that would prove effective must treat his physical, mental and spiritual disorder at one and the same time.

The fortunes amassed by the Carnegies, the Mellons, the Fords and the Rockefellers have been largely diverted to the welfare of man generally, yet their pooled resources multiplied thousands of times would not accomplish the good that resulted from the heritage left us by the Poorest Man that ever lived.

The power of wealth as compared with the power of Love is puny to the point of being unworthy of comparison.

If your pockets are not lined with gold but your heart is, you can still be a power, not only for this generation but for those yet unborn.

Our sobriety is dead-serious. It has to be, to work at all. With it we can retain all we now have, and the limits to which we can add to it are circumscribed only by our initiative and our ability. Without sobriety we are in danger of losing that which we already have.

Sobriety is life itself to us and without it life would again become a living death. To unnecessarily subject ourselves to temptations is another variation of playing "Russian Roulette."

AA is not fundamentally a philosophy, but it is rather a program of active living. To commit the Big Book to memory, to listen attentively to all the group speakers will not guarantee continued sobriety.

The knowledge gained thereby, put into your everyday living, will make drinking practically impossible and certainly unenjoyable. If we fail to make the Program an integral part of our everyday living, we are almost sure to have some rough times ahead.

Exactly what is AA worth to you? Have you ever figured that out? Make a written list sometime of the benefits you have derived from your sobriety. Try hard to make an honest evaluation of what it would be worth to you in dollars and cents. How much have you benefited mentally, spiritually, physically, financially, socially?

Then make another list — how much has AA benefited by your membership? Are you trying to give as much as you have received? If not, you are getting something for nothing and that isn't honest. You can never square the debt but you can probably give it a little better try than you have been doing.

To pity distress is a natural human characteristic, except in the case of the poor drunk. The hospitals want no part of him. He brought it on himself and besides they need their beds for really sick people. Many doctors won't make a house call if they suspect the patient has been drinking and when they do, their medication consists for the most part of something to knock him out and keep him quiet. People who spend hours raising funds for the tubercular and the cancerous call a cop when they see a drunk.

God knows the drunk and He also knows human nature, and so He invented AA.

We are very apt to travel in the direction we are headed. Even the brightest of sunshiny days appears overcast if we wear black glasses. If we enter a restaurant by the rear door we will undoubtedly find garbage cans, smoked and grimy walls and hear the discord of pots and pans. If you enter by the front door you will find cleanliness and order.

Let us enter each new day by the front door.

A sinner is usually a sinner because he is thinking wrong, whereas a mean person has a warped and deformed personality.

A sinner's faults usually lie in his thoughtlessness, but the mean person is nearly always a person of strong will and determination.

Sinning stems from weakness, meanness from strength.

A dog will love a sinner but seldom a mean person.

We not only are judged by our words and actions, but also we are frequently misjudged by them. If you do or say anything at all, you will be either judged or misjudged and the purity of your motives will not affect the verdict.

Therefore take but little thought of the judgment of men but in all things strive to earn the commendation of that still, small voice within you.

In our drinking days there was no humor in the world except that doubtful brand we heard around the bars. It is certainly true that we took our insignificant affairs and our ridiculous selves most seriously.

In AA, when we became mentally sober, we not only acquired a sense of humor but we were even able to laugh at ourselves. We can now accept the criticism of others with a greater degree of patient good humor, we have learned that the best way to confound our critic is to laugh off his attack with good-humored tolerance.

It is not possible to help a man as long as he stands in his own way, nor can anyone or anything else.

A vast host of drinkers could quit if they could get a job, but they can't get a job because they are drinking.

They could quit if they could get their families back but they can't get their families back because they persist in drinking.

We are all too prone to get a new man "fixed up" so he can stop drinking instead of making him realize that he must stop drinking so he can "fix himself up." He must get out of his own way first.

It is often the case that great scholars make the acquiring of knowledge a goal instead of a means to a goal.

If you thoroughly learned all the lessons in AA by heart and made no use of it you would find it but a waste of time and effort.

You must put your new-found knowledge to work, you must pass it on or it will be not only valueless to humanity but, in all probability, of no material help to you.

Youth might be termed a zest for living. As long as we have enthusiasm for living we are young, regardless of years. Too often the alcoholic has taken so many hard knocks from life that life has lost its attraction. We have seen so many hopes and ambitions fade that life appears to us a total loss.

AA brings into our lives a new purpose in living; it restores our faith and hope, and thereby rejuvenates our minds to the point of a new zest for living.

Remember those days when we were
SMART; when we knew our way
around; when nobody could tell us
what to do; when we actually felt sorry
for the dumb SOB's who labored every
day and took their pay check home to
Mama?

In those days, the world had chosen
up sides; we were on one side and
everybody else was on the other. We
would work them for all we could; they
in turn kicked us around at every opportunity.

Frankly, fellows, who was actually
smart and who dumb?

The spoke that is on top of the wheel will be, in half a revolution, on the bottom and in the mud. Another half turn and it will be on the top again.

The same applies to us alcoholics. We, too, have our cycles, but in the AA Program we have acquired a faith in ourselves, a reliance on our fellowship and a belief in a Power Greater than Ourselves that enable us to take our bad along with the good in full knowledge that if we "stay right" everything will turn out right eventually.

As a piece of machinery deteriorates faster when standing idle so it is with the Soul.

It is a law of Nature that any faculty that is not used is taken away, and the more it is used the stronger it becomes.

An active Soul is a healthy Soul and the various functions of the body are so arranged that it is not possible to have physical and mental health without spiritual health and strength.

Many of us alcoholics can withstand the big trials but succumb to life's petty irritations. We are like the mighty big-game hunter who survived many harrowing experiences with wild beasts yet lost his mind when he sat on an ant hill.

It is not too difficult to remain cool during a great crisis, but a fouled up shoestring can throw us off the beam.

Columbus is the only man on record who didn't know where he was going when he set sail, didn't know where he was when he got there, and didn't know where he had been when he got back, and still escaped the reputation of being an alcoholic.

If AA paid no further dividends than to get us out of that haphazard, confused and disordered way of living, it would be enough.

Now we at least know which end is up.

In all ages men have been bound to each other by the ties of kinship, nationality, mutual attraction and by common ideals and aims. Nowhere, however, is that bond of kinship so strong as among those who share a common danger.

We in AA have a common enemy in Alcohol. It is a constant threat to our happiness, our prosperity, our health and our very lives.

Here lies the reason behind that feeling of "belonging" when you enter the halls of a strange group. Here are your kind of people, fighting your battle against your enemy.

It is most fortunate for us arrested alcoholics that we can never know the price we paid for our former dissipations.

One man received a splendid promotion about a month ago, and was told that his name had been considered for the job for fourteen years but that it had been held up because of his drinking.

There is no use in crying over spilt milk — those days are gone forever and carried their opportunities with them — but today is here now.

Suspicion, and its first cousin, jealousy, are the world's most bitter poisons. They are compounded from surmise, rumor, and malicious gossip and are mixed in the retort of confused and unsure minds.

They serve no useful purpose on earth, but they torture all who possess them. It is much better for a person to have his worst fears justified than to live with unproven suspicions.

We alcoholics devoted a whole lifetime to the pursuit of happiness, but it was not until we found our fellowship that we had any success of a permanent nature.

This is a happy Program, made so by our happy release from the Hell of drinking excessively. Our happiness distinguishes us from the dried-up drunk.

The work we are about is dead serious, but we can go about it with a smile in our hearts and a laugh on our lips. Of all God's creatures we really have something to be happy about.

We in AA are taught to live for today and to shut out all regrettable yesterdays. This philosophy is good, but
it does not mean that we can cut off
yesterdays as though they never existed.

If we had not been alcoholics in the
yesterdays, we would not be in AA
today. If our lives had not been
wrecked, we would not now be rebuilding upon a better and surer foundation.

We do not need to lament over mis-
spent yesterdays, but we should salvage
what was good in them to help con-
struct our new way of life.

It is not possible for man to live without emotions, and all emotions are passions. Emotions are as good as our control over them. Even those which we look upon as bad are bad only because they are not under proper control.

The Creator of man endowed him with emotions as part of the necessary equipment to live a full and useful life. We live our lives and enjoy them only to the extent we curb and regulate our feelings.

God put nothing evil in man. Man has diverted his blessings to evil purposes.

It is frequently true that many of us might be better employed. A lot of good farmers and mechanics have been ruined by making doctors, lawyers or engineers out of them.

When we finally sobered up, many of us were unemployable in the profession or trade for which we had some aptitude, and the necessity of getting a job made us take the first thing that presented itself.

While we are on our Inventories, it might be well to check on our adaptability to our present jobs and where we are wrong endeavor to do something about it.

In our drinking days we had sufficient knowledge to know that there
was a better way of living, but it was
beyond our wildest imaginings that such
a life was possible for us. An idea that
sprang from the imagination of Bill and
Dr. Bob took root in our minds, and we
became possessed of the knowledge that
enabled us to convert our lives into lives
beyond the limits of our imagination.

In all great emergencies, people instinctively turn to the man who has complete control of all his faculties. Few indeed are the difficulties that we can fight our way out of, yet few indeed are the difficulties that we cannot think our way out of.

Confusion is unknown in the mind that is cool, calm and collected.

To the new persons on our Program who might be confused about the Moral Inventory, it would seem that for a starter, it will suffice if they will sum up each night their actions on the past day. If their honest appraisal of that day meets their approval, if it is definitely better than the days preceding, then actually the Moral Inventory is in operation whether recognized as such or not. If daily you are making a moral study of your thoughts and actions your defects will be noticeable and you will instinctively take steps to correct them.

Those of us who have our drinking tamed do not necessarily have our thinking or our actions under control. We are not under control until all our actions are under the domination of our intelligence, and our intelligence cannot properly function until we have thoroughly schooled it into instinctive sober and sane thinking. This constitutes one whale of a big job, one that will last a lifetime — but we can start on it today.

We alcoholics feared loneliness as much as anything else on earth. Even the companionship of the bull pen was preferable to being alone. The quality of our company made no difference, for it was preferable to our own thoughts; certainly, it was not as critical. We just couldn't stand our own company.

In AA we were told to establish conscious contact with the Man Upstairs and we marveled at the ease with which this was accomplished after a little effort on our part. Now we are never less alone than when we are alone.

Last year I attended the Southeastern Convention at Miami Beach and I had a grand time. Yet I do not recall, offhand, the name of a single speaker I heard, but I do remember the name of the man whom I called upon as a Twelfth Stepper.

I fretted somewhat, at the time, that this man caused me to miss several meetings of the Convention, yet today it is MY highlight of the affair. This man is happy on the AA Program and I am happy that I was forced to forego some of the pleasure I travelled all the way to Miami to enjoy.

Poverty will often force a man into sobriety because of the lack of funds with which to purchase more to drink. Prosperity on the other hand gives us the money, the leisure and inclination to celebrate that prosperity.

Far too frequently the new man climbs out of the gutter, gets a job and becomes re-established with his family, and does well until a payday puts cash in his pocket again.

That bank roll which you think you want may be the very thing you least want.

Patience is a virtue that few alcoholics have. We want to do everything yesterday. Even after we sober up, we seldom acquire any substantial amount of this virtue. We feel a real need to make up for all our lost years; we fret and fume over delays; we feel the world should synchronize their watches with ours.

Like Phillips Brooks, we are in a hurry, but God isn't.

Everything you can buy with money will either die, rot, wither, evaporate or decay. There is nothing you can purchase that will surely last as long as you will, unless it be bad health.

Friends can be bought, not with money, but by a liberal expenditure of yourself. A dollar is a poor weapon to fight off real troubles.

God is Good and the truly Good things of this life were put here on earth for our use by Him and not one of them carries a price tag.

In AA we must of necessity make the best use of our time. The hours must be allocated to our various affairs in proportion to their importance. We now have so many responsibilities we did not have in our drinking days.

If we wisely divide our time between our duties to our families, our jobs, our community, our God, and getting our own lives in order, we will find little time left for worry, fear, self-pity or envy.

Humility has been the hardest of all the virtues to acquire for many of us. Few of us know what it actually is. Many have it and think they don't; many don't have it and think they do. Many admit they don't understand the word and forget it, leaving to the world to judge whether they have it or not.

The best way to acquire Humility is to constantly remind yourself how much lower than a snake's belly you would be but for the Grace of God. You made a horrible mess of running your life and failed completely but that Grace could and did, make you what you are today.

No pleasures of our drinking days ever compensated for those horrible nights of wakeful tossing. The interminable pacing the floor; those night sweats; the endless hours when we couldn't sleep and at the same time dreaded falling asleep. The hours that seemed to stretch into eternity as we lay in bed with remorse as a bedfellow. Then the Hell of the goof-balls that made our nights better and our days worse.

The physical pain we might have endured for many more years, but the anguish of the heart and soul was unendurable.

In our drinking days, we were ready to take a poke at anyone who suggested we couldn't handle our "likker." It was a very sore spot with us, as we all kidded ourselves into believing that our over-indulgence was a well guarded secret, when actually we knew it was not.

Upon our entrance into AA, we soon made a public confession of our alcoholism and, to our surprise, we lost some of the sense of stigma and we could learn to laugh at our affliction and at ourselves. Our sense of guilt was lessened by our acknowledgment of its existence.

It has been observed by many in AA that the surest bet to get our Program is the man who needs it most desperately. His very desperation lends strength to his efforts. He has been backed up to a wall and he must fight his way out of his dilemma or else he must die. There is no alternative.

Only the coward quits in despair, and the alcoholic can't be a coward, for if he was, he would have quit the unequal game long before his alcoholism was fully developed.

Yes, it takes a brave man to fight his way to the gutter and it takes a brave and desperate man to fight his way out.

The very basis of AA is kindness to the suffering alcoholic, but the question often arises as to what is the kind thing to do. Sometimes we have to do things that might be considered cruel in order to be kind.

There are occasions when it is an act of kindness to have a man locked up if he is apt to hurt himself or others. Sometimes drastic steps have to be taken to prevent a man from driving his car when he is drunk. Occasionally it might be the best thing for a man if his boss should fire him or if his family left him.

We are frequently called upon for this kind of advice. Who are we to decide such issues? God has the answer and it is best to turn the query over to Him.

The educated person knows things but the wise man knows people. It is not possible to know life without knowing the individuals that make up the world.

A man is not a thing — he's a combination of certain good and bad traits that make him distinctive among his fellow men. Each one is an influence for good or evil, whether we realize it or not. When we rub elbows with our associates, we exchange some of our characteristics with them. Watch, therefore, your companions, for if they are unclean they are sure to soil your clothes.

It is almost a general rule that no one achieves in life what they planned in their youth. The great ambitions of our teens never seem to materialize.

In spite of all our plans, it is a safe bet to say, however, that we are where we were intended to be, doing the things that we were intended to do, whether we like it or not. Apparently we are not running the world.

It is very probable that we would have made a terrible mess of it had we followed our wishes and would have wound up a much bigger flop than we did. No matter what our station in life, we can daily thank God that it is no worse than it is.

In our drinking days, when we were called upon to face a problem, we would side-step it, tunnel under it, jump over it or run away from it. It never occurred to us to face it and to walk through it.

It is remarkable how cowardly a trouble is when face to face with a person who is ready and willing to take him on. Try it.

It is not natural for a human being to be entirely contemptuous of public opinion. We all smart under criticism and we all enjoy applause. We cannot be blamed for purring like a cat when our fur is being rubbed the right way.

Neither public acclaim nor public censure is always deserved, however, and we should therefore temper our reactions to them until we have received the stamp of approval from the little man inside us, who really knows the facts as to our deserts.

Service ends one of his verses in this fashion, "it's the keeping on living that's hard." Living has always been hard, not only for the alcoholic, but for humanity in general, since the beginning of recorded history, and was probably even worse before that.

We are surrounded on all sides by people who find living all too rugged for their puny strength. This is our opportunity. We find we can lighten their load of living and, curiously enough, we find that we lighten our own loads in so doing. Living then becomes less hard for us and assumes a sweetness that appears divine in its richness.

Some of us wear our AA like we wear our clothes, entirely as external adornment and protection, and to hide what is underneath.

There are many, however, who wear their AA in such a way that the AA way of living is so predominant in their appearance that all other apparel is unnoticed. To see such a person, the reaction is not to observe a gray suit or a blue dress, but a personality that radiates a character made beautiful by the simple code of living as found in our Twelve Steps.

In their first efforts to grasp the Program, the new men are very frequently at a loss as to how to begin. They feel they have been so wrong in their attitude toward God and man that it appears that they have a multitude of things to do, when actually it can to a large degree be combined into one short sentence — act toward your fellow man as though God were watching and toward God as though man were watching.

As it is almost impossible to remain entirely anonymous, our membership carries with it grave responsibility.

Once we were drunks and we "ain't any more." All your friends and neighbors know it. Sooner or later they will ask you about it and if you answer them at all it is probable that you will have to admit your membership in our Fellowship.

We will be watched constantly thereafter, for AA is on trial with a hopeful yet skeptical world, and as we succeed or fail so will AA succeed or fail.

Guard your anonymity well, if you can, but, if you can't — then guard AA well.

None of us has ever personally known a person who died and surely went to Heaven. As all men are sinners, we are told, then it is assumed that even the saintliest of men have some hidden sins in their past, either of omission or commission.

We do know of many cases however, of people who have died the living death of Alcoholism and who have come back to make a little Heaven here on earth for themselves and all those around them.

Many of the uninformed non-alcoholics looked upon us of the Drinking Fraternity as lazy bums. They do not know the planning and scheming required to raise the price of a bottle when you are broke. They fail to realize that a twelve-hour shift of panhandling frequently didn't produce enough to keep us in booze, a little food and a flop for the night.

We resent the charge that we were lazy — we worked much harder and received much less appreciation for our efforts than those who were on somebody's payroll. No, it is hard work, small pay and lousy living conditions.

The men and women who are doing the bulk of the work in your Group seldom complain. They are too busy doing their job and yours to have the time. There is no time left for griping.

If things are not being run your way, maybe that is because you are doing nothing to "change the things you can."

If you are one of those who think they are unable to speak at meetings, or to do a little Twelve Step work, then give a try at some other AA activity. If you have a phone you can always call up some new man and shoot the breeze with him. If you have a car you can arrange to pick up some guy who hasn't got transportation and bring him to meetings. Or you gals can occasionally baby sit for someone who wants to attend meetings but can't get away.

There are lots of things you can do if you try. You once thought you couldn't quit drinking, but you did.

Frequently people who are only sober in AA try to carry our Message to other alcoholics without realizing that if you have only sobriety you can only carry sobriety. In order to carry the AA way of life you must live the AA way of life.

The fact that you are sober doesn't imply that you are on the Program. In fact, many outside of AA have longer periods of sobriety behind them than anyone in AA. They started before AA was started. Whether in or out of AA, if you have sobriety only, you are a dried-up drunk in my book.

The older some of us get in AA the more we notice a tenency on our part to become a little bit less tolerant, a little less understanding in our relationship with the man still having trouble. We have been so long removed from the actual suffering that we are losing some of our understanding.

This is a good time to pick out the messiest case we can find and get back in the groove again. We can't afford to forget that we too are alcoholics and but for the Grace of God we would be in just as bad shape.

We may be years away from our last drunk but we are only one drink away from our next one. Don't lose the common touch.

As startling as this may sound to some members, AA has no first, second or third class memberships. A sober member is in good standing if he has been dry for twenty-four hours or twenty-four months.

Of course, no one means to discriminate, but some of us just naturally gravitate to a certain person or group of persons within the group. The "low-bottoms" are just as guilty as the "high-bottoms" in this respect. After all, we were all drunks and all of us smelled the same when we came in.

Filth and dirt were the things we were trying to avoid when we climbed out of the gutter. To get physically out of the slime and still leave your mind wallowing in it will inevitably lead to trouble. You have only succeeded in getting your body on the sidewalk if your head is still in the gutter. You should get your feet with your head in God's clean air to insure sobriety.

To do something about your habits without cleaning up your thinking is like taking a bath and neglecting to wash your dirty feet.

The newspapers announced that Doctor Bob died on November 19th, 1950, but we of AA know different. He lives today in the grateful hearts of three hundred and fifty thousand alcoholics and probably three times that number of dependents of alcoholics. He will live forever for he was the founder of something Good and Good is eternal.

His name would be out of place in cold, hard stone, but it is engraved forever in the hearts of a grateful and growing multitude.

Some time ago, I felt it necessary to make a record of the various sums of money owed me for my occasional handouts for a flop, or to get clothes out of hock, or to replace the false teeth lost or broken on the last binge. The total amount began to grow to staggering proportions and I became very unhappy — so unhappy, in fact, I tore the record up and now I am happy again.

There is no man alive who is a bigger fool than he who knows everything — even God can't teach such a one. This characteristic is common among alcoholics, and constitutes one of the greatest barriers to recovery. Our Program is best received by the humble heart and the attentive ear.

We must do a lot of "un-learning" before we are ready to start learning this new way of living.

Had Doctor Bob died in May 1935 he would have died a failure — a man who had wasted years of training and exceptional ability, a despair and a disappointment to his family, his profession and himself.

But Doctor Bob lived for fifteen more years, and accomplished more in that short span than the combined efforts of his entire profession in the treatment of the baffling disease of Alcoholism.

Medicine had treated the drunk like a guinea pig. Dr. Bob looked into the heart and soul of the man. He soon learned that the physical aspect of the case was the least and most temporary of the causes.

Alcoholism is now recognized as a disease, and this recognition brought about countless studies and experimentations on the part of the physicians, scientists, educators, employers, etc. Clinics are being set up, new medicines, new cures, new therapeutics are being experimented with. There are almost as many theories as there are alcoholics. There are almost as many failures as there are theories.

Alcoholics Anonymous is no theory, it is a proven fact.

When a member of AA can take his first inventory and compare it with his last and then truthfully say, "I am not now that which I have been," he has arrived at a definite stage of improvement. When the next one shows still more improvement, then he is definitely on the Program. When this improvement continues until there is no more room for improvement — look out below.

If we think — truly think — our lives will become manageable, and if we thank God who made this thinking possible for us, then our lives are almost sure to remain manageable. We alcoholics can contain our entire philosophy in these two words — THINK and THANK.

Think before you take that first drink, then thank your God that you didn't.

With fiery zeal we devote much energy to going through the motions of living AA. We speak on every occasion we are invited, we rush ourselves dizzy carrying the message to all who call on us, but in the process we sometimes neglect the one man we are most interested in — ourselves. Our AA has become muscular.

To reach ourselves requires quiet meditation, daily use of prayer and a comprehensive study of the Program and of ourselves.

Everyone agrees that excessive drinking is an evil. The alcoholic is convinced that for him it is a necessary evil. He thinks he would surely die if he didn't drink. We know now that it only appeared necessary while we were doing our thinking with our appetites.

No evil is necessary except in the sense that friction is. Without it, we couldn't get traction and without traction we could not move onward and upward.

The subconcious aim of practically all men is to get the most and the best out of every day of their lives. It is a simple creed and if honestly followed, day by day, act by act, it cannot help but lead to greater heights.

Like AA, it is so simple it is incredible. Why not try it? It's what you honestly want anyway.

The relationship of hours to a lifetime is comparable to the relationship of bricks to a house. Every brick that is laid must be a separate and distinct operation, yet so tied to the preceding and the following brick that their positions are level and plumb. Each one is an entirety in itself but all the bricks are either supporting or are supported by each other.

Our hours, lived one by one, are in no sense different. The beauty, strength and durability of our lives will be determined by the individual hours viewed collectively.

You can't swim like a fish, run like a deer, fight like a tiger, or fly like a bird. Every one of your five senses is excelled by some member of the animal kingdom. Man, physically, has many superiors and would long since have been extinct but for the fact that he alone possesses reasoning power.

With this advantage he can build ships to outswim the fish, motor cars to outrun the deer, perfect weapons to outfight the tiger, and airplanes to outstrip the fastest of birds. With this reason he can visualize the reason behind all Nature and thus avail himself of a Power greater than himself and all the forces with which he has to contend.

It is a constant source of amazement to some of the Old-Timers to answer a call for help from some alcoholic and to find that the person in trouble is a neighbor, relative, friend or fellow employee of a member of AA.

It sometimes happens that the new man preferred it that way as he would rather discuss the matter with a stranger than someone near him.

It is also true that some of us are not quick to grasp the opportunities to pass the Message along. If you see a man is beyond his depth and can't swim, why should you wait for him to yell for help? He might be deaf and dumb.

The alcoholic is usually conscious of his shortcomings but he resents any well meant attempt to discuss the matter with him. He knows that has no defense. Logic is against him; lying frequently backfires on him and is therefore unreliable. He has but one avenue of escape and that is the bottle, the very thing the well intentioned friend is trying to avoid.

Our only approach that makes sense to him is the visible evidence that we are doing it, and acquainting him with the fact that it can be done.

The secret of cutting any tree down, regardless of size, is to hew it one chip at a time.

Men are not put in a position to do great things until they have established the reputation for doing many small things well.

If you have the great ambition to bring happiness to a whole world, a good starting point is within your own undershirt.

Faith is probably the first natural virtue that the human being acquires. A baby's reaction to its mother is different from earliest infancy. It is an instinctive faith that this one person, above all others, can and will supply all its needs. This faith in mother decreases as the child develops and becomes more self-reliant. He loses faith in the parent as he develops faith in himself. Finally he arrives at a point where he depends upon himself entirely. When Alcoholism develops and he begins to lose faith in himself, he feels completely helpless.

He must then start rebuilding faith, first in the Group or his Sponsor, then in the Program itself, and finally in God. When this is accomplished then faith returns in himself.

Too many of us ex-drunks expect too much when we get dried out. We, with characteristic impatience, see no reason why we can't, overnight, regain all our lost ground and get the fifteen thousand dollar job that other sober men get.

Drying-out only gives us the opportunity to realize our ambitions. Ability always has been, and always will be, a factor to be reckoned with. Getting sober won't make a musician out of a boilermaker.

If you are a person who likes his drink and yet has to forego his pleasure in order to retain some semblance of order in your life, you will naturally be miserable.

For you there is but one remedy. Get busy on the Program, talk it, work it, preach it, think it, pray it, live it — then you will find that you like it.

The amount of compensation you get for your labors depends on the value of the currency, not the denomination of the bills. A million dollars in Chinese coin would break your back carrying it, but might not buy you a suit of clothes.

The greatest compensation would therefore be that which would buy those things which you need and want.

For services rendered your fellow men, God gives you his I.O.U., and they are better than cash on the line in any currency.

Remember those days when you walked around with a chip on your shoulder — daring any and all the hostile world to knock it off? Well, they did knock it off, and you were beaten and kicked at every turn. You were constantly fighting alcohol, and people, and things.

The day finally came when you had had enough; you were beaten to your knees; the chips toppled from your shoulder when you surrendered, and your burdens became lighter at once. Actually you had only been fighting yourself all the time.

In our introduction into AA we were admonished "Easy does it," in order to guard against the evil of trying to swallow more than we could digest. There is so much to AA that there is always the danger of taking an overdose. The wise AA doctor prescribes for alcoholism as a physician would for tuberculosis, very little medicine to be taken internally, but lots of fresh air and sunshine to be absorbed from day to day.

There can be no improvement in the world without the improvement of the people who constitute it. There can be no improvement in people unless it is in improved actions motivated by improved thinking and a higher morality code.

Aside from the immediate benefits derived by the alcoholics and their families from the AA program, it has done much to raise the character of a large segment of society.

Charity would be absolute foolishness if this life was the beginning and ending of all things. If there were no closer relationship between men than between animals, then we would be animals.

We know, however, that a mystical bond does unite mankind, and it is best exemplified in the practice of charity. As it lifts man above the level of animals, it also lifts man closer to the angels.

We are attempting to build a new house on the site of the old wrecked one. The type of house we build will be determined by the plans and specifications we select. Exactly the same materials can be used to build either a palace or a hovel; the difference will be chiefly one of design. The palace requires more material and a great deal more labor, however.

In your rebuilding be sure that the basement is DRY; the corners SQUARE; the walls UPRIGHT and TRUE, and your house will stand, even after you, the builder, are dead and gone.

If the price we paid when we took a drink was the only price we had to pay, it would not be too expensive. It was the terrible price we had to pay after the drinks that really put the screws on us. For $3.50 most any bartender will contract to deliver you ten drinks of whisky but the busted-up car that results can run the costs up to a first class funeral.

In spite of evidence to the contrary, we still persist in wondering what would happen, after our several months of sobriety, if we again took a drink.

We definitely know that we don't want "a" drink. We never did in our drinkingest days. We know that we have graduated from the ranks of happy drinkers. We know of no one in all our experience who has made the experiment to his or anyone else's satisfaction — yet we *might* be the exception.

It is this type of curiosity that has killed many a cat. Don't try it. Even if you are right — you're wrong.

Beauty that only appeals to the eye is shallow and is of short duration. A thought is only beautiful if it inspires beautiful action. A masterpiece of painting is a masterpiece only if it inspires people to beautiful thinking. Mechanical perfection is only good craftsmanship unless it provides a need for humanity.

A thing of beauty is one that serves a beautiful purpose. If your actions are not motivated by lofty ideals and purposes you are denying yourself much that is beautiful in life.

The greatest battles of life are won or lost without the sound of a single shot. Suppose Christ had lost His battle with Satan at the time of His temptation? Its repercussions would have been greater than all the battles of history.

Your greatest victory, your greatest display of courage in your fight against Alcohol was not accomplished amid flying banners and the flourish of trumpets but in the quiet of your own heart.

The most courageous thing a man can do when he has fought a good fight and realizes that he is up against unconquerable odds, is to admit that he is whipped. General Robert E. Lee's reputation for courage suffered not one bit by his surrender at Appomattox.

The main objective in talking is to say something, not just anything. Words give a truer picture of a man than does a photograph, for words are reflections of the inner man, beyond the range of the finest camera.

Most of us alcoholics have been hurt more by our own words than we have by the words of others. Let us screen our words through our minds and give expression only to those words that are products of a sober and thinking intellect.

Many people in AA take too literally the statement they hear to the effect "we have no initiation fee or dues."

Alcoholics Anonymous is not free — it costs a whale of a lot. It takes your time, your money, your thoughts, your prayers. It will give you a lot every day of your life, but it also requires a lot of your everyday living.

If you are stingy with AA, you are cheating yourself.

If you want a horse to work for you, you must feed him.

A deep stab wound must heal from within outward, or fresh tissue would grow over the lip of the wound and prevent the necessary drainage from beneath. Blood poisoning would set in and the poison would circulate through the entire body.

Human improvement works the same way. If it is only a surface cure, the poison remains in the heart and mind, affecting our entire life, and unless moral surgery is resorted to, our characters become infected.

The AA Program is moral surgery, wherein we remove sick and diseased thoughts and actions from deep within ourselves and thus become entirely healed.

The cry of the single word "Help" will bring more people to your rescue than a long and eloquent oration of your needs. If the God of your understanding is a personal God, one who has all Godly attributes in infinite quantities, then He knows your needs before your sluggish human intelligence is capable of realizing them. The secret of prayer is not long or frequent appeals in Biblical phraseology but an humble, contrite heart, a hope that expects its plea to be heard. A recognition of the Infinite Love that we acknowledge will do all those things which He, in His wisdom, knows are best for us.

The troubles of the backwoods mountaineer are just as big and just as numerous to him as yours are to you. They seldom crack up mentally, however, because they have no "experts" to cure them of their present worries by finding things wrong that they never suspected before, thus giving them a brand-new crop of worries.

We often worry ourselves into the psychiatrist's office and then worry ourselves into another when we get the first one's bill.

If most of us had one wish, we'd wish we hadn't had it. Most of all our difficulties in the past resulted from our persistence in doing what we wished. To us alcoholics our wishes were paramount and everything else was sacrificed in order to accomplish them.

From here on in, if we are smart, our wishes will be, not what we want, but a sincere desire to want what God wishes.

We alcoholics had contracted the world until it was no larger than ourselves and our narrow interests. We had few interests that extended beyond our hand or our eye. Everything else was relegated to another world entirely apart from us. It is little wonder that the world gave us no more thought, except for our nuisance value, than they did a man from Mars for, we too, were occupants of another world.

In Step Twelve, we learn that we should "try to carry this message to alcoholics" but only after we have "had a spiritual awakening as the result of these steps."

Notice, please, that it does not say that we have an "understanding" but it says "spiritual awakening." It takes no English scholar to know the meaning of every one of those two hundred words. A child of ten can grasp what the words actually say, but it is only when we have had this spiritual experience can we understand their full significance.

Only when we have this spiritual experience do we fully possess the Program, and unless we possess it, it is certain that we cannot give it away.

We are all serving a term here on earth, and it is a tough rap for we are not only serving a life term but we are condemned to death in the end. We can get some special privileges for good behavior, however, but even with this it would be a hopeless situation except for the hope held forth in the inspired Book of God.

Through this Book we can look forward beyond this prison of Life and visualize the freedom that is beyond.

Everyone is potentially as good as God made him and the reason that he does not show it is because he has buried the fact beneath a mountain of selfishness.

It has ever been man's misdirected efforts to benefit himself and himself alone that have resulted in his greatest disservice to himself.

The closer man gets to himself the further away he is from God and the world. The further he is away from God and the world, the further away he is from God's blessings and the world's happiness.

Famous Last Words: "If I had one more drink I could cut off." "Lord, get me off this one and I'll never touch another drop." "A glass of beer won't hurt me." "I'm sober, ain't I, I don't need the meetings." The list is too long to go on.

We constantly sell ourselves a phony bill of goods and then cry our eyes out when we find we have gypped ourselves, but — it wasn't our fault, understand? If the wife hadn't — , if the boss hadn't — , if, if . . .

For us alcoholics, the First Step in life was the usual toddle of the infant. The Second Step we learned to walk erect like a man, the Third Step, we started to run to keep up with the world, the Fourth Step we were staggering, the Fifth Step was stumbling and falling, and the Twelfth Step found us erect again.

What happened between the Fifth Step when we fell and the Twelfth Step? Don't ask me, I'm an alcoholic too, I had probably just blacked out. Watch your steps — they take you places.

We have all had the pleasure of knowing intimately several men who might be classed as "Gentlemen of Leisure" and what a squirrel cage they were usually in. They labored all night long to get in jams that required a staff of lawyers all the next day to extricate them.

It takes a big man to make effective use of leisure.

We members of AA have a tremendous responsibility. We must in our work discuss the most personal matters with the new guy or gal. This information is given us under desperate circumstances and should be treated as most confidential. Carelessness in this respect can and does do a lot of harm at times. Let us confine our conversations with each other to only that part of the new man's problem that pertains to his actual drinking, because that is the only phase of the problem that we can efficiently advise him on, anyway. These personal matters are matters of trust and they deserve the same confidential treatment as a church confessional.

Our AA philosophy is an idealistic philosophy. It has to be in order to be a happy philosophy. Some may declare that it is too much so, that we ignore more materialistic facts. Let us take from our philosophy all the good and the joy it promises. Let us give our gold no acid test.

If our philosophy is unreal and foolish in the eyes of the more materialistic world, then what of it? It enables us to be happier than those that have good sense.

Somewhere we read that alcoholics made their own bedlam and then lied out of it. This has not been our experience. We made our own bedlam, it is true, but unfortunately we were usually stuck with it. Somehow we could never successfully lie out of it. Lying somehow always failed and on the few occasions when we did get by with one, we were forced to tax our feeble brains for the balance of our days to guard it and not expose ourselves. A liar must of necessity have a good memory or he's sunk.

Most of us have met persons whom we thought extremely homely until we knew them better. Then we ceased observing their lack of facial beauty and began to appreciate those persons for what they really were.

George Washington and Abraham Lincoln were what might be called extremely homely men, yet the beauty and strength of their characters was such that practically all present day pictures show little of their ugliness.

You can't do a whole lot to improve an ugly face, but you can hide it behind a lovely character.

Promises, vows, pledges, resolutions, doctors, preachers, priests, psychologists, psychiatrists, hospitals, judges, jails, jitter-joints, in fact everything, but nothing worked.

One day, by the Grace of God, we found ourselves sober, and there can be no denying that it was the Grace of God alone that caused it. That same Grace will remain with you as long as you honestly seek it, and you will find that it will prove more than sufficient.

You cannot sell a man a bill of goods without selling yourself. This is the experience of all those who speak at meetings or attempt to carry the message to other alcoholics.

Whether your talks help the other guy or not, you may never know, but your efforts have not been in vain for you will have undoubtedly helped yourself in the attempt.

The opportunities around us for doing good are so numerous that to do all the good things we would like to do is almost impossible. Nor is it necessary to read the papers for opportunities to help. They are near at hand and far more numerous than we suspect. Our eyes see what they are trained to see and a little practice will enable them to see many opportunities that you once failed to observe.

If your prayers include a request to never let a day go by without some opportunity of serving, you'll have your prayer answered and you will rejoice in the fact that you have so much to do, and your lone regret will be that you cannot do more.

Prohibition is a glaring example of the futility of endeavoring to protect men from their own follies. The setting up of barriers is effective only in challenging the resources of man to overcome those barriers.

It is an unfortunate truth that we never fear a hot stove until we have been burnt, and a fresh paint sign serves only as a dare to everyone to put their finger on it and see for themselves.

We alcoholics should be the last people on earth to give advice; first, because we never took it ourselves, and secondly, because our past record would not indicate that our advice is trustworthy.

The best advice that we can give is to show the new man that we did it, show him that he can do it just as we did it, that the best way to get "on the Program" is to emulate the example of those who have made a success of theirs.

A shipwrecked sailor on a desert island may eventually find another in a like predicament, but the poor alcoholic is all alone with himself, even in a world full of alcoholics.

That is one of the most brutal characteristics of the malady that separates us from the world about us and makes us men without a country, without a hope and without a friend.

So you killed the goose that laid the Golden Egg? That's too bad. You can't bring it back to life but you can do the next best thing—you can eat the goose. You can't unscramble an egg but you can bake a cake.

It is water going over the dam that drives the machinery. You are an alcoholic—you can't help that fact, but you can use your alcoholism for the benefit of other alcoholics and society generally.

Who can estimate the Mozarts, the Shakespeares, the Edisons, the Raphaels or the Jeffersons who stumbled through life in an alcoholic haze and achieved no greater acclaim than the title of "Drunken Bum." Many may have arrived at a drunkard's grave with their talents remaining unsuspected. Their bodies died before their souls began to live.

You may never be a world-beater yourself, but you may say a word to someone else that might revolutionize his life, and that life may revolutionize the world.

We are not in a position to give an opinion on leprosy, jungle fever, hoof-and-mouth disease or other minor ailments like that, but when it comes to the really "big sickness"—hang-overs—we can speak with some authority.

How any piece of mechanism could take the rough treatment we gave our human bodies would make it appear, on the surface, that Nature intended to make us live to punish ourselves in a manner that Nature itself could not duplicate. Outraged Nature could only confine its retribution to the body. The mental and spiritual beating we took was administered by ourselves. That was the most cruel of all.

There can be no liberty for any man unless he is free, and he can never be free as long as he is a slave to anything, save God himself.

If a person subjects himself, body and soul, to the Will of God, then he is indeed free, for then God resides in him and he in God. They become to a more or less degree one and the same. Blended into a perfect oneness above all earthly domination and as free as God himself is free.

What will be the ultimate result if AA becomes too attractive? It is felt now that some people are joining our ranks, not because they have a major drinking problem, but because they fear they have alcoholic tendencies. Our meetings are interesting, friendly and informative. Will AA degenerate into a Social Club and cease to be the last refuge of the suffering alcoholic?

Will we find eventually that we have too many "enjoying" AA and too few fully appreciating the "responsibilities" that attend our membership?

The bootleggers in Prohibition days devised the very worst tasting concoction ever devised by man, added alcohol to it and sold it to us and we drank it.

Remember the routine? First we would shudder from stem to stern; then hold our breath and throw it down; then we would cough and choke nearly to death and after wiping our chins we'd say "Damn, that's good."

If you could sell yourself that kind of a story, selling yourself on the idea that you don't have to drink should be a cinch.

AA has no formal textbooks—we learn by absorbing the experiences and the wisdom of those who have successfully found an answer here. The rate of our progress in AA is to a large extent dependent upon the ability to listen and to digest what we hear.

We may not be conscious of acquiring any degree of wisdom at the end of any one meeting, but when we look back over a period of a month or so, we see that the things that entered our ears have taken root in our hearts.

By the very nature of our AA work, we often are exposed to the worst in the new man on our first contact with him. Too frequently, we pronounce judgment at once, and all our future work is prejudiced by that first impression.

Think back a little — you weren't a lily yourself when you sought AA.

In your AA talks you may have the eloquence of a Patrick Henry, but if your AA work stops there, you are only fooling the new man temporarily. He will soon get wise to the fact that you are but a phonograph, nice to listen to but of no use to anyone beyond this one function.

Beautiful sentiments need lovely actions or they have but little value. Lovely actions speak for themselves.

The life of the alcoholic is very similar to a jigsaw puzzle. In our days of drinking, the whole of life appeared as simply a jumbled mass of unrelated pieces, impossible to unscramble.

In AA someone gave us the corner piece and from this we slowly and laboriously found one piece after another. Each piece that we fitted in made it easier to find the next piece.

First we found understanding, then hope, then determination, then sobriety, then unselfishness, then love, then faith and finally God.

All the pieces are in place finally, the picture makes sense and it is beautiful to behold.

Bad luck is not often just a series of unhappy events that just happened. Our bad luck is usually the result of our ignorance, carelessness or indifference.

Our experience with bad luck should make us more careful and then good luck can be expected to follow in consequence.

It was your bad luck that brought you to AA; it was your good luck that you profited by it.

For a person who knew almost everything just a few years back, and who now knows more than he did then, it is indeed strange to have had that consciousness of just beginning to learn the most elementary facts of living.

One day, not too long ago, you lost everything in the world you held dear, then a man sat down with you and he gave you friendship, understanding, faith, hope, courage and opportunity. Have you ever realized the great value of what this man gave you? These were the tools with which you made a new and better life.

Someone did this for you, so "go and do thou likewise."

We alcoholics should never claim Justice. It is the one thing in the way of a virtue that we can't use. It would be poison.

It would be found upon examination that had we received justice we would never have gotten to the door of AA. The warden wouldn't have allowed it. If we are wise we will confine our conversations to Mercy, for this is something we want and need, but if Justice was ever given us in full measure we would find it would be something we didn't want.

"Why can't that guy get the Program? He is down and out, he has taken a terrible beating, just what is the matter?"

We try to analyze the man, his mental capacity, his home life, his employment, his environment, and the answer just isn't there.

Have we improperly delivered the message?

The chances are he isn't ripe—he still wants to drink.

He cannot see the light, but he is probably further away from it than you think. Maybe it just isn't dark enough yet.

Resolutions, like clay pigeons, are made to be broken. They are nearly always made in sincerity, but the very act of making a resolution is a confession on the part of the maker of his inability to keep it otherwise. As resolutions are contrary to the subconscious wishes of the maker, they are almost surely doomed from the start.

If a person really wanted what he resolved, he would do it without the resolution, for we are prone to do those things that we really want to do.

The greatest piece of self-deception on the part of the drinker is the actual belief that a drink will make him feel better. We got this illusion because alcohol in the blood stream and in the brain deadens the misery mometarily, but it also served to make us thirsty and so we continued the drinking and inevitably felt worse. Whisky will pick you up a foot or so but it drops you a hundred. What made you sick will never make you well.

All men eventually die, it might be said that we live to die. The way we die is usually the way we live. Dying is the last thing we do on this earth, but certainly we do not live just to die. Living would not be worthwhile if that were so.

The only worthwhile purpose of living is that those whose lives we come in contact with will be enriched thereby. If you live so that others will live more abundantly then you are performing the purpose of your little life.

Gifts are usually given for favors already given or for favors expected. Even the sudden outburst of affection from friend wife, is frequently followed by a glowing description of a dress she saw downtown.

The gift of AA is one exception. We give AA away because it is the only way we can keep it ourselves.

Carrying your own troubles may be likened to a man trying to pick up a board that he is standing on. He has his own weight to contend with as well as the weight of the board.

It is much easier to carry the other man's burdens for we are standing away from the problem. We can view the problem impersonally and thoughtfully. We can show him where he is standing in his own way, direct him to take hold of his end of the problem and allow us to lift the other end. The weight, distributed between the two of us, will become relatively easy to handle.

We human beings are no more miraculous than the ape organically. We do not even have some powers possessed by brute creation — for example, we cannot change color at will as can some reptiles. We can't change our physical make-up as the tadpole does when it becomes a frog, or a caterpillar when it changes into a butterfly.

Yet we are the miracle of all miracles. for we alone have a soul, which enables us to transcend this planet and commune with God himself.

Each and every one of us have what we have only by the Grace of God. Even if we acquired all our possessions through our own industry and intelligence, still you must admit that you gave yourself none of these attributes that made your acquisition possible.

These were not necessarily inherited traits, for geniuses have had morons for children. You have what you have because God so willed it, so use them as God would will it.

The Founders of AA acted wisely when they fixed it so there would be no Big Shots in our fellowship. We are not the best people in the world when it comes to bearing heavy responsibilities. It has proven to be poison to many a good man.

After all, it is not necessary for your fame to spread around the world—there are more drunks on your own street than you can help.

If life is only a preparation for something yet to come, as many believe, then the manner of our living will determine the success or failure in this preparation. It would naturally follow, therefore, that a man could not live a devil and die a saint.

We do not feel that we are qualified to evaluate the worth of deathbed repentance but this we do feel—if you live right, deathbed repentance would hardly seem necessary.

Have you ever visited the General Service Headquarters in New York? Do you have any conception of the vast amount of work that passes through the Foundation every year?

It is highly possible that your Group would not exist today were it not for them. It is likewise probable that if your Group did not exist you would still be beating your brains out.

The New York Office is functioning beautifully but they require the support of every Group to do so. Make it your business to see that your Group is doing its share.

Our philosophy of living does not reach as far as immortality—it concerns itself with living this life one day at a time.

We do feel, however, that if we live this day to the best of our ability, endeavoring each day to improve over the preceding day, then when the time comes for us to consider immortality, we will be in a very favorable position, to say the least.

A large number of people come into AA antagonistic to Churches, yet most everyone recognizes the fact that Churches have a vital role to play in the development of civilization generally.

If religions are not what they ought to be, it is because we are not what we ought to be. The Church's failure is man's failure. Man is the culprit that relegated spirituality to second place behind creeds and dogmas.

Instead of Churches leading men, men are leading Churches.

One of the first things we should endeavor to do is to kill the lawyer instinct in ourselves. In our effort to get the new guy straightened out we try to cure all his troubles by giving advice on subjects on which we possess neither the training nor ability to talk constructively.

Let us confine our efforts as far as possible to those things of which we have real knowledge — his sobriety and the AA Program.

According to St. John, God is Love. That appears to be the only description given and leads us to assume that it is His chief attribute. The fact that things are not always as we think they should be does not contradict it. Practically all our griefs we brought upon ourselves, many of them were essential in order to fully develop our characters, and many may be the result of God's long-range planning that we with our limited perception, cannot conceive.

If God had not loved the world, He would have given up on it a long time ago.

Every one of us alcoholics arrived at the point where we felt that all was lost. If we had not felt this way we would never have confessed that our lives were unmanageable. It was a stupendous admission for us and would never have happened except for the desperation that engulfed us.

Our lives had been totally wrecked, it is true, yet God has never yet failed to give man a second chance. Don't muff it.

It takes two people to make a fight. Everybody will not be against you unless you are against everybody — including yourself. If you are at war with the whole universe, it is because a civil war rages within your breast.

If you so live as to be able to like yourself, then peace will reign in your life and your attitude toward everybody will be free of fear, jealousy and suspicion. You will have no reason to oppose anyone and none will oppose you.

It is a most comfortable feeling for us alcoholics to know that there is a vast host of friends in AA who are standing by. We pray to God we will never need them for an *emergency* and, with our new-found faith, we don't think we ever will, but it helps a lot to know that they are available if needed. It gives you a feeling of security akin to catching the fourth ace.

We are all subjects to the habit of imagining a lot of needs and desires that we would not actually want if we stopped and gave the matter some thought. List those needs sometime and then think them over carefully. A yacht would be mighty nice in the summer but it's a pest in the winter. A fat bank account takes more thought and hard work to keep than it ever did to acquire. It is much nicer to just let your friends have these things and you be their guest.

You are born at every sunrise and die at every sunset. Sleep is temporary death, which fortifies you for your rebirth in a new tomorrow. Every day is an entire life in itself and all human experiences can take place within its span.

You, yourself, are not the same man you were yesterday or the man you will be tomorrow. The world, too, changes with every revolution around the sun. One human being lives a day and another a hundred years yet each is a complete life.

Today is the only life you surely have. Make the best of it.

No one ever became noble simply by being moral. The great characters who have had their ennobling influence pass down through the ages are those who lived, labored and died for others.

Nothing endures that fails to serve a useful purpose and man, individually or collectively, is no exception. We must be of constant service to humanity or we are useless members of society.

You not only pass through this world but once but you live this day but once. The opportunities this day presented to do good are lost opportunities tomorrow unless you grasped them in passing.

Your greatest personal loss in your drinking days was not material but rather it was the loss of many hundreds of opportunities to do those things which make life worth living to you and those about you.

Those opportunities are gone forever, for you will never live those days again — but you are living today.

It is one of the peculiar characteristics of the alcoholic that he almost invariably shows the worst side of his disposition to those people for whom he has the highest love and respect.

Many of us were Jolly Good Fellows in the bootleg joint but Hell on wheels at home and in our relationship with those we loved.

If your disposition is so lousy that it isn't fit to be brought out on the street, then it isn't worth house room.

Fortunately, sobriety usually cures this.

We alcoholics were accustomed to look at the world through whisky glasses and consequently what we saw of the world made it appear as one big case of D.T.'s.

Sobriety corrected our vision and the world took on a more ordered appearance. The world hadn't changed — our viewpoint had.

If the world still doesn't look good to you — probably you are still looking through your old glasses.

We become too easily discouraged when the new man fails to make the grade. What we fail to keep before us is the fact that we are not accountable for the results of our efforts. We are only charged with the responsibility of carrying the message to other alcoholics.

Just go about your end of the job, which is sowing the seed, and if the ground is fertile, God in His good time will bring forth the harvest.

All forward steps in the progress of civilization have been the results of great ideas. All advances in the field of science were first ideas, many of which were conceived years before they became realities. Their creators were thinking far in advance of their times.

Alcoholics Anonymous is not a new system of ideas but it is rather a new application of old ideas whose time has come.

Money is a medium of exchange and is as good as the things you can get with it.

If you have enough money in your pocket when you fall overboard it can drown you.

Love of money can make you the most despised of men, but love of mankind can make your money a blessing to you and to them.

A large segment of humanity, stumbling in alcoholic darkness, resigned to a belief that nothing can possibly be done about the situation, has at long last caught a gleam of light and presses on to that beacon of Hope.

Alcoholics Anonymous is that light shining forth in the night of despair, and your hand holds the torch. Be sure you hold it high, that all suffering alcoholics may see it, and direct their faltering steps over the proven pathway that you trod.

Man has within him something that is higher than man, and we can lift ourselves beyond our physical and human status in becoming absorbed by the highest instincts in ourselves.

Man is mortal, it is true, but you surpass man when you live in strict accordance with the Godlike characteristics you possess.

If a reasonable estimate could be made of the fatalities resulting from excessive drinking, the figures would be appalling. This loss, however, is only a small part of the price that Bacchus exacts.

The wasted man-hours of work, the homes broken up, the wealth of talent that was never developed, and the loss of moral character are also a part of the bill.

You definitely can't drink moderately. Can you afford to drink to excess?

Moderation is not an alcoholic's strong point. Few improve much after joining AA, they simply direct their energies to other activities but with the same amount of intemperance.

"Easy Does It" is a nice sounding slogan but seldom do we see any great display of it among the members. They usually jump into their jobs with increased enthusiasm or they find an outlet for their energies in AA work. It is probably for the best, however, for excessive activities are not as prone to make a man return to the bottle as too much inactivity.

Isn't it strange to note the absence of a lot of our old pre-AA friends over the week-end? We have not offended them, surely, and we are just as good friends as we used to be, but somehow, they don't call on us with the same regularity. The answer is simple — the bar is closed.

Now home is what it should be and the people who do call do so because they like us and not just to get a drink.

Every practicing alcoholic is firmly convinced that the Devil has all the good tunes. It was the music we had wanted and the tunes to which we had attuned our ears. His music was louder, more catchy and, to our thinking, was prettier. We suspected, however, that it did not have the soul-satisfying qualities that make good music.

We must learn all over again to train our senses to appreciate those things which are really good and not cheap imitations.

Probably the first permanent benefit we received in AA was received when we undertook a personal inventory of ourselves. Then for the first time our faults were dragged out into the open where we could meet them face to face and endeavor to do something about them.

Had we not recognized these defects we would never have taken steps to eradicate them. It is dead certain that if we still had them in the same degree, we would not now be sober. It was a definite step toward getting wise to ourselves.

In our drinking days, fear of everything and everybody was our constant companion. These fears continued until we finally, in desperate necessity, found the courage to surrender — to quit unconditionally. Then we found AA and a ray of Hope. Hope became desire, desire became determination. With necessity as our charger and with determination as our lance we were adequately armed to overcome our despair.

Sorrow and happiness are mental states, but the effect they have upon our nervous system and our blood pressure is a recognized fact.

The "Atmosphere" of a hospital and its staff can lengthen or shorten the duration of an illness.

We alcoholics spent years driving nails into our coffins; let us spend today drawing those nails out.

Knowledge is of great value and nothing of value is acquired without price. Wisdom is even more to be desired than knowledge, which can be but an accumulation of facts. Humility is greater than wisdom for there is no real wisdom without humility. The wise are humbled by the knowledge of the limitations of their knowledge.

No man is born with these characteristics, they are born of the vicissitudes of life. Sorrow, despair, and failure are their breeding grounds.

We find in life exactly what we are looking for. In your drinking days you courted trouble constantly and you probably found more than your share of it.

Today we are looking for a better way of life and this, too, we find at every turn.

We get what we want if we put forth sufficient effort to look for it, if we have the ability to recognize it when we see it, and the tenacity to hold on to it when once we grasp it.

Many who are active in AA work come to feel that they just can't carry on any longer. There is so much to do; so little time can be spared to do it; so few to do the work. There is a limit to their edurance. After all, a guy has just so much health. strength, and patience.

When the burdens get too heavy and too numerous, take it up with the Big Boss, tell Him you like to do His work, but that it is more than you can handle — ask Him for more help — you'll get it.

There will always be a difference of opinion as long as people have different interests, different prejudices and different mental capacities.

To expect people to disagree with you is only sensible and reasonable. If everybody agreed with you, everybody would be as smart as you and you wouldn't like that for a minute. The chances are you are both wrong anyhow, or you would not be required to defend your opinions. The right can defend itself without your help.

Fires, floods, and epidemics are no-body's business — they are everybody's business. Alcoholism is equally devastating and just as much a community catastrophe.

We in AA are unique in that we are trained veterans in the art of combating this disease. Its prevalence demands the complete co-operation of every qualified man or woman, and we are guilty of dereliction of duty and lacking in gratitude to the Grace of God that saved us, if we do anything less than our utmost.

I feel good today and I ought to. I slept like a baby last night, had a fine breakfast that I relished, the wife and kids kissed me as I left the house, I arrived at the office whistling and didn't give a damn whether the boss was in a good humor or not. The work, too, seemed so much easier to do and the gang in the office seemed so much friendlier. It's payday, too, and I drew a whole week's pay and I haven't borrowed a cent from a soul in the office. The whole envelope can go home unopened.

AA gave me all this. To me, an alcoholic, this IS Heaven.

Sometimes people say, "I tried AA but somehow, it just didn't seem to work for me." They had lost faith in the Program but a careful analysis of the situation would show that they had not been faithful TO it. No medicine will cure a sick man unless he takes it regularly and according to the doctor's orders.

You will, have no occasion to lose faith in the Program if you live faithfully to its precepts.

A man once ridiculed me in front of a large class in school and I have hated his guts ever since. That was thirty-five years ago and I do not know whether he is dead or alive. If he was aware of my intense dislike it certainly never bothered him but it certainly bothers me even now. His face springs up in my memory and I begin to hate him all over again. This situation is just pure dumbness; I'm not hurting him but I am distressing myself.

God teach me to forgive as I hope to be forgiven.

If you are satisfied with your progress in AA you are not only an exception, but you may be headed for trouble. Remember One Day at a Time, and Easy Does It. Before you measure your advancement, be sure you have an accurate yardstick. Nature is always slow in its development of good things.

Some weeds mature and bloom in a few days, but it takes Nature many centuries to perfect a diamond. Don't worry about your rate of progress — you have a lifetime ahead of you — but just be sure that you progress.

Every person at some time in life has a spiritual experience of some kind. It may have been no more than a soul-stimulating experience after hearing a beautiful hymn, beautifully sung. Perhaps it is only an undefined hunger within when viewing alone a star-studded sky, or an awe-inspiring view. Maybe it was experienced when looking upon the miracle of a baby.

The soul of even the most callous will light up when it glimpses the beauty and power of God.

Have you ever noticed those old expressions: "Sit down and cry"; "Prostrate with grief"; "Wallowing in pity"; "Bowed down with troubles," etc.?

Truly troubles in all their forms get us "down" so the only antidote would appear to be to "get up and do."

Remember when they used to tell us, "If you don't stop drinking you'll go straight to Hell"? What a laugh that is — trying to tell us about Hell when we had been living in it for years. If we had told them about the Hell we knew, it would probably have scared them into drinking.

It is hard for us at times to understand the misfortunes that befall us when we are doing the very best we know how, to live right by both God and man.

It is only in times that try men's souls that the soul develops and grows stronger. Like a muscle, it develops with hard work.

If you would produce an exceptional rose, you must prune the brush of every budding branch so that all the strength goes into the single bloom. It's not what the bush would want, but it develops the perfection in the rose you desire.

Every man is both human and divine, both good and evil, strong and weak, wise and foolish. The body, soul and mind are the battleground of our conflicting natures, and while these conflicts rage, we can have no peace.

It is only when we bring our conflicting emotions under control that victory over self is possible. We alcoholics have learned that we are unable to accomplish this without outside help. With that help, real peace is obtainable. No other way has worked for us.

If our God. as we understand Him, is a personal God, then it is reasonable to assume that He is so close to us that He is residing in us. He is then part of us and we are part of Him. As we cannot have two different personalities at the same time, we can assume we are either worldly or Godlike, depending upon the characteristic that has dominance at the moment of any specific action.

We cannot expect this God in us to help us unless we are in accord with Him and are endeavoring to help ourselves; otherwise we would be working contrary to ourselves.

Give the God in you a chance — He has given you a thousand.

One of the great satisfactions resulting from sobriety is the ability to drop into bed at night with the knowledge that the day has been completed, all chores finished and no regrets.

There will always be affairs to be taken care of on the morrow, but we know that tomorrow will find us physically and mentally prepared for most any eventuality. Remorse and Fear are no longer our bedfellows.

Our greatest enemy was alcohol and we have learned how to protect ourselves against it, but we are in constant danger from some of our well meaning friends. They constantly tell us how wonderful we are in that we have cut out our drinking and, unfortunately, we sometimes believe them to the point where our heads begin to swell.

At that very moment, that very necessary ingredient of sobriety, HUMILITY, goes out the window and sobriety frequently accompanies it.

Faith is a fundamental requisite of success in retaining our sobriety — faith in God, faith in the Program, and faith in ourselves.

It can be likened to swimming: Every normal person can swim, if he has faith in the laws of buoyancy and allows himself to be submerged enough. Those people who cannot swim are those who are afraid of the water and try to raise themselves above it.

Faith in the laws of Nature and in yourself enables you to swim, and a like faith in God, the Program and yourself, will enable you to achieve our way of living.

Every alcoholic has at one time or another had such a load of troubles that there was surely no prospect of his ever being happy again.

On the other hand, there were moments of ectasy that were so great that our lives seemed completely filled and no cloud could ever possibly enter our lives again.

Both conditions existed only a brief while, until another mood appeared. Both, to a great extent, are products of our state of mind. Unhappiness can be guarded against and happiness can be cultivated.

The world is a looking glass; it returns to you what you give to it. All the world and everything in it are but reflections of yourself, and if the world doesn't look good to you, rest assured, you don't look good to the world.

The words of every person you meet are but an echo of your own, and wherever you go the world will be the same unless you, yourself, change.

We must work out our spiritual development in our own way and according to our conception of the God of our understanding.

Our success or failure will be determined by the honesty of our efforts and the fidelity with which we practice our convictions.

It is very difficult for an alcoholic to remain sober in continued idleness, and this lesson has been learned the hard way by too many who have tried it.

It is also possible to overwork to the point where we think we need a stimulant to keep going.

There is a big difference between resting time and idle time. Rest is necessary, but that does not imply that resting time is idle time. A hobby, as an illustration, may be restful and yet be strenuous. Some of us have been so exhausted from our daily work that attendance at AA meetings was dreaded, yet we forced ourselves to go and the diversion caused us to leave the meeting rested and refreshed.

Any constructive program of living is a process of character building that lifts us above commonplace worldly affairs to the higher sphere of the soul.

In this way, the house of the soul becomes the temple of the God in us, a cathedral of the spirit, where you and God mutually reside in love and harmony.

If the purpose of living is to live so that our lives will be more like that Divine Example that God has disclosed to us, then only our deeds in life can serve as our advocate at the bar of Infinite Justice.

It will be our deeds that will speak for or against us, and we will be judged worthy and well qualified only if our actions so testify.

It is frequently distressing to observe the attitude of the slipee when he sobers up and endeavors to get back on the Program. Some apparently think it was something to be expected, others feel that it was a necessary part of their alcoholic education and that their slip makes them full-fledged members. Still others take the attitude of "So I slipped, well, what the hell of it?"

They ignore entirely the fact that they have injured AA, as well as themselves. And how about the guys who had to neglect new men, possibly, in order to sober them up?

Every kind deed, every noble act pays off double. You get your first pay-off the instant you do it, provided, however, that you did not perform the act just for the pay-off. It will give you a bang that a shot or a goof-ball can't approach.

The second pay-off comes later on, for no human action is exempt from repercussions. The world must eventually react to any act, good or bad, and the bread you cast upon the waters will be returned to you on some later tide.

Did you ever think upon forgiveness as a Christmas Gift? In addition to its sacred application, the giving of gifts at Christmas is to bring happiness to someone and nothing can bring more happiness than forgiveness. It gives joy both to the giver and the receiver and must also bring a smile to the face of Him who said "it is more blessed to give than to receive." It depletes your purse not one penny but adds materially to spiritual wealth.

At some time in your AA experience you will be called upon to make a talk before the Group. When that time comes, remember that you are talking for the new man out in front. You definitely are not talking just to demonstrate your wisdom and your oratorical ability. Above all, you don't exaggerate your story nor make statements that are manifestly untrue. It has been done and the effectiveness of the talk destroyed. Keep in mind that the man out in front is an alcoholic and he can spot a phony afar off.

As we alcoholics are selfish by nature it is but right and proper that we should be more severe in our judgments of ourselves than of others. As we are our own best friend or our worst enemy, depending upon our treatment of ourselves, and as we are the one person in the world from whom we cannot escape, it is therefore essential that we do not allow ourselves to get away with anything in our treatment of ourselves. When we forgive ourselves we are rationalizing, but to forgive others is divine.

The average person has so much trouble in finding a satisfactory faith simply because the mind has difficulty visualizing a force so powerful as anything but a very complex thing. He thinks he must understand it in order to acquire it and use it.

When we eat a meal we believe that we shall digest it and that we will be strengthened and sustained by it. Yet few of us know the mysteries of the digestive functions, but we get just as much sustenance from our meals as those who do.

We therefore eat our meals on faith and we would probably ruin our digestion if we tried to figure it out.

It is very often easier to identify an alcoholic by his hang-over than by his drinking pattern. Alcoholics, for the most part, resemble the non-alcoholics when they have a load aboard, but in the mornings, when the sweats and the shakes set in, then the alcoholic can be identified by the degree of his suffering. The alcoholic's hang-over cannot be gotten rid of by ten-thirty simply with aspirin or Bromos.

Is someone happier, better, or braver because of some act of yours today? If you can answer yes to any or all of them, then you can feel rather confident that you are progressing in the AA way of living.

If you can't — then you are not giving it the old College try and you are cheating yourself out of a lot of happiness that could have been yours.

If man was created by God in the image of God, and did not possess human frailties, he would be God. All men would then be perfect and Heaven would exist here on earth. There would be no logical reason for it to operate simply as a branch of Heaven.

With our limited understanding of God's purpose, we must suppose that man was intended from the very first to work out his own evolution. The reason this process has required so many centuries has been man's persistence in the exercise of his puny little will as opposed to the Will of God. That we are less than God is due to our freedom of choice between being one with God and our attempt to play God.

Every man at some time arrives at a place where the course of his entire future rests upon a decision. Judas was one day a saint and the next he was the betrayer of his Lord.

We members of AA also had our moment of great decision. Many more days of decision will probably be our lot, but by the Grace of God and our new-found sobriety, we can meet any situation by reliance on God's Will rather than our own.

About Hazelden Publishing

As part of the Hazelden Betty Ford Foundation, Hazelden Publishing offers both cutting-edge educational resources and inspirational books. Our print and digital works help guide individuals in treatment and recovery, and their loved ones. Professionals who work to prevent and treat addiction also turn to Hazelden Publishing for evidence-based curricula, digital content solutions, and videos for use in schools, treatment programs, correctional programs, and electronic health records systems. We also offer training for implementation of our curricula.

Through published and digital works, Hazelden Publishing extends the reach of healing and hope to individuals, families, and communities affected by addiction and related issues.

For more information about Hazelden publications,
please call **800-328-9000**
or visit us online at **hazelden.org/bookstore**

NOTES

NOTES

NOTES

NOTES

NOTES

USD $19.95   CAD $26.95

ISBN: 978-0-89486-023-2

51995

9 780894 860232

Order No. 1020